SOCIAL WORK AND THE WORKPLACE

About the Author

Dr. R. Nalini was conferred her Doctoral Degree in Social Work by the Department of Social Work, University of Delhi. Presently she is Faculty Member, Deptt. of Social Work, Pondicherry University (A Central University), Puducherry.

SOCIAL WORK AND THE WORKPLACE

R. Nalini

CONCEPT PUBLISHING COMPANY PVT. LTD.
NEW DELHI-110059

The Publication was financially supported by the ICSSR. The responsibility for the facts stated, opinions expressed or conclusions reached is entirely that of the author and the ICSSR accepts no responsibility for them.

The work was evaluated by Professor Surinder Jetly, Former Professor, Department of Sociology, Banaras Hindu University (B.H.U) Varanasi on behalf of the ICSSR.

ISBN-13 : 978-81-8069-777-7

First Published 2011

Published and Printed by

Concept
Since 1974

Concept Publishing Company Pvt. Ltd.
Regd. Office:
A/15-16, Commercial Block, Mohan Garden
New Delhi-110059 (India)
Phones : 25351460, 25351794, *Fax* : 091-11-25357109
Email : publishing@conceptpub.com
Website: www.conceptpub.com

Editorial Office:
H-13, Bali Nagar, New Delhi-110 015, India

Cataloging in Publication Data--*Courtesy:* D.K. Agencies (P) Ltd. <docinfo@dkagencies.com>

Nalini, R.
Social work and the workplace / R. Nalini.
p. cm.
Originally presented as the author's thesis (Ph. D.)--University of Delhi.
Includes bibliographical references (p.) and index.
ISBN 9788180697777

1. Tata Group. 2. Social responsibility of business--India. 3. Industrial welfare--India. I. Title.

DDC 658.3820954 22

Dedicated
To

Sudha, my loving Sister

&

Balaji, my loving Brother

Preface

Workplace has been one of the legitimate areas of social work intervention since the early days of professional social work practice in India. Social Work has been an integral part of the efforts promoting employee well-being in the world of work. However, it is not to be regarded as a panacea to solve all performance problems in an organization, nor should it be regarded as an exact science designed to solve all human misery.

Tata Group, one of the oldest in India, has around 98 industrial organizations. The study was carried out in six industrial organizations namely – Titan Industries Limited, Hosur, Tamil Nadu, Tata Infotech Limited, Mumbai, Maharashtra, Tata Motors Limited, Pune, Maharashtra, Tata Refractories Limited, Belpahar, Orissa, Tata Steel Limited, Jamshedpur, Jharkhand and Tata Tea Limited, Munnar, Kerala. Further, the study has included major sectors – engineering, steel, FMCG, plantations and information technology.

In India, labour welfare has been one of the major areas of social work practice since the beginning of social work education and training. The need for welfare services grew with gradual growth of industrialization and it was shaped by different factors and forces affecting the organizational structure, quantitative and qualitative changes in the workforce, degree of unionization, state intervention and regulation and development of management sciences. In 1948, the Factories Act enacted specific provisions for the appointment of Labour Welfare Officers whose qualifications were also laid down under the relevant rules. The rules incorporated, *inter alia*, Master's degree in Social Work with specialization in labour welfare and industrial relations as minimum qualification for appointment to this post. Though specialization oriented social work has continued to exist mainly because of availability of employment opportunities in diverse fields, it has been a subject of debate throughout, leading to division among social work educators.

Later, the human resources development approach, which was more akin to social work philosophy and values, broadened the scope of social work practice in industries. "Social work practice promotes human well-being by strengthening opportunities, resources and capacities of people in their environments and by creating policies and services to correct conditions that limit human rights and quality of life" (Mohan 2003, p. 113). Social work professionals in industrial organizations are engaged in varied positions performing different kinds of functions ranging from labour welfare, employee relations, personnel administration, employee counselling, community development, employee assistance and corporate social responsibility. However the issue of desirability of social work practice in industrial setting is still a matter of debate.

Tata Group has pioneered social work interventions in the field of labour welfare in India. The well-being of their employees has been a major concern of Tata organizations. Tata Steel has been a pioneer in introducing many firsts in the area of employee welfare, counselling, employee assistance programme, corporate social responsibility, social auditing etc. Some of the welfare firsts of Tata Steel such as eight hour working day, free medical aid, establishment of the welfare department, leave with pay, workers' PF scheme, workmen's accident compensation scheme, and maternity scheme etc., introduced as early as 1912 became rationales to enact legislative protection by national and state governments. The main aim of this research was to explore social work practice in its various forms in select industrial organizations of Tata Group of industries.

In the **first chapter** titled *Social Work Practice in the Workplace*, an outline of social work practice in industrial organizations in India and other industrialized countries has been presented. In the backdrop of work and workplace, the human factor in industry and the changing profile of industrial workforce, the growth and development of social work practice in industrial setting in Indian context has been discussed. In the Indian context, industry also has a social purpose as it is not only an economic organ of the society but has a social purpose as well. This social purpose is partly a derivative of social cultural forces and partly assigned to it by the state. Most of the social work practices are essentially agency sponsored. However, as already stated, the industry is typical among the agencies in which social work is practiced.

Qualitatively, there is major difference between the characteristics of workforce of yesteryears and the workers of the present period of post-globalization.

The **second chapter** on *Social Work in the Indian Workplace* has examined the historical background of social work practices in the Indian workplace. Historically, the genesis and growth of the social work practice *vis a vis* the profession in industry can be briefly categorized in five phases on the basis of its characteristics: Initiation Phase (prior to 1936), Integration Phase: (from 1936 to 1952), Inclusion Phase (from 1952 to 1975), Innovation Phase (from 1975 to 1990) and Imitative Phase (from 1990 till date). With history of more than one century of unionization, government interventions and employers' statutory and non-statutory welfare efforts, workplace and the workforce have undergone tremendous changes in its dimensions. The steady flow of fixed income enabled establishment of basic living standards for the worker and his family. As Datt & Sundaram (2005) observe,

"Only in recent years, a new class of industrial labour without roots in agriculture is emerging in our towns and cities. With widespread technological revolution shrinking the globe as village has definitely increased

In the West, occupational social work grew as a specialized intervention to respond issues related to work, worker, and workplace. In India, social work practice is still limited to welfare aspects of employees and their families but social work professionals are increasingly required to respond to corporate social responsibility. Social work practices are fast becoming an integral part of the world of work.

The **third chapter** is on *Review of Literature*. The researcher has reviewed studies both from West and India. The review of literature in this study addresses the area intersecting social work and industry especially labour welfare, personnel management, industrial relations, human resource development, training and development, working with unions, industrial counselling, occupational social work, employee assistance programme, corporate social responsibility, working with specific groups etc. The review revealed that there are not many studies directly addressing social work practice in industry, in West as well as in India. Select researchers have studied social work practice in industry in India at different time periods. Interestingly, most of these studies were done for higher research degree by social work educators in India mostly by women. The review indicated the following trends: (i) Scanty research on relevance of social work education in industrial setting, (ii) lack of exclusive study on the practices of professional social workers in industry.

An analysis of this chapter indicates that the feasibility of social work practice in industry has been debated across the globe for many years now. While earlier labour welfare was considered social work in industry, the trend has changed with new concepts emerging in human resource development.

The literature review indicates the need to study the nature, extent and types of social work practice in select industrial organization of Indian conglomerates with a tradition for social work and the professional social workers working in these organizations. Therefore, there are gaps in the theoretical knowledge about the problem under investigation, which has necessitated this study.

The *Profile, Perspectives and Practice of Select Industrial Organizations of the Tata Group* have been discussed in **fourth chapter** with the purpose of understanding the background in which Tata Group crystallized its philosophy of welfare. Tata Group is one of India's largest employers in the private sector inspired by the spirit of nationalism. Jamsetji Nusserwanji Tata, the founder, launched the famous Empress Mill and Swadeshi Mills, pioneered India's first steel industry; started the first power plant in India; pioneered civil aviation in India; brought insurance to India; started India's first chain of luxury hotels; led commercial vehicle production; initiated India's software development efforts; produced India's first passenger car and introduced labour welfare benefits long before they were enacted by law.

The main aim of the Tata Group is to improve the quality of life of the communities it serves. The founder of the Group believed that "our heritage of returning to society what we earn evokes trust among consumers, employees, shareholders and the community. This heritage will be continuously enriched by formalizing the high standards of behaviour expected from employees and companies". The five core values of Tata Group are: Integrity, Understanding, Excellence, Unity and Responsibility. The principles behind the Group's social initiatives sprung from its concern for nationalism, which paved the way for their corporate philanthropic activities. TCCI (Tata Council for Community

Initiatives) was established as a result of the need felt within the Tata Group to co-ordinate all Tata Companies in meeting their social responsibilities. The Tata Group has evolved a CSR index, known as the *Tata Index for Sustainable Human Development* to benchmark the contributions of Tata companies toward social development and protection of the environment. The core values of the Tata Group are concerned with the development of employees on the one hand and societal development on the other. Towards employee development, the Tata Group has gone beyond the statutory welfare measures adopting progressive and proactive human resource management practices. An analysis of the strategies of the Tata Group indicates that employee development and social development are being integrated into the long-term goals of the organizations.

Tata Group has been a pioneer in implementing welfare programmes in their organizations that too voluntarily. Even before the government assumed the role of welfare state and entered into legislative protection, many welfare provisions of different legislations were in practice in Tata Group of industries. Thus, the Tata Group has the unique distinction of introducing welfare measures that were at that point of time non-statutory, but later on became guiding lines for government action.

While statutory welfare ensures good working conditions and conditions of work, Tata organizations have initiated various programmes within and outside the workplace not covered under statutory provisions. Some of the significant programmes are: Employee Counselling, Loans/ Small Savings, privilege leave in anticipation, upgrading knowledge, healthy life programme, higher education, encouraging adoption, rehabilitation committees etc.

Family has also been the focus of the attention of Tata philosophy of welfare. Family planning had been the area of intervention till 1970 and later on the focus progressed to family welfare. In all spheres of life, there are special groups seeking assistance and are in need of special care and protection. Some of Tata's programmes for special groups are: Employment opportunities to the disabled, Srishti Complex a training and rehabilitation centre for the children of employees found to be mentally or physically challenged, Developmental Activities in Rehabilitative Education, Domestic Management Programme, Community Welfare, Community Based Business Opportunity etc. Besides this it has partnership project with government like (Tamil Nadu Small Scale Industries Corporation Limited), TELCO Grahini Udyog, Tata Relief Committee and Life-line Express. Tata has developed policies, programmes and guidelines on social issues such as drug de-addiction, HIV/AIDS, equal opportunity employment, employee volunteering scheme, Social/Welfare audit, HR practices and organization development.

Social Work Professionals and Practice in Industry has been discussed in the **fifth chapter**. This Chapter is based on the primary data from social work practitioners in industrial organizations.

Professional social work interventions have travelled a long way from welfare approach to right based approach; from welfare amenities to personal need care activities; and corporate philanthropy to corporate citizenship. PSWs are engaged in performance of multiple tasks in the areas of labour welfare, industrial relations and HR management. Among labour welfare functions, majority is engaged in community work/corporate social responsibility, implementing welfare programmes and other statutory welfare duties; in the area of industrial relations, they are engaged in implementing grievance redressal, employment standing orders, managing unions and discipline matters. Training and development is one of the major areas where an overwhelming majority is involved. Most PSWs are performing multiple tasks directly involving the employees.

Most of the PSWs are engaged in some form of activities related to industrial social work at various levels – policy-making, drafting programmes, implementation, evaluation etc. which in turn depends on their positions. All the primary methods of social work are used by PSWs in varying degrees as per their job requirements.

As far as linkages in social work practices by PSWs in different departments are concerned, there are many commonalities and interactive reinforcement on each other. differences can be seen in three different angles: (i) individually, (ii) between PSWs in the organizational hierarchy and (iii) nature of activities/functions performed.

Since industrial organizations are competitive, result producing and fast, the PSWs felt that they have to work under 'pressure to produce quick, tangible, results' in executing their responsibilities, followed by lack of clarity among other colleagues about professional social work, as well as to work in contradiction to social work ethics.

An overwhelming majority admitted that they have scope for applying social work methods/principles and this is a matter of interest considering the debate on applicability of social work in industry. Professional social workers agree that social work training increases their emotional intelligence. Principles of social work are claimed to be effective in understanding and empathizing with individuals and groups. Respondents felt that faith in the development of people makes one realize that social work is possible irrespective of settings.

Another significant area of social work practice, which has been mentioned by a good majority, is developing individual employees including training and development, organizational behaviour and leadership. Crisis response is an area of social work practice for more than half the PSWs. Core HRD, employee welfare and life services were perceived by PSWs as an area for social work intervention. Educational counselling for the children of elderly employees, for instance was taken up. Privacy concerns of the employees (clients) were handled effectively due to social work knowledge.

An overwhelming majority has pointed out the relevance of social work in industry because of changing nature of human/organizational problems, human aspect cannot be ignored, employees in any organization will have specific problems and specific problems require specific professional intervention. On their future prospects, an overwhelming majority felt that the role of the social worker in industry is to promote Human Resource Development (HRD), industrial relations, and working with the community in and around the workplace. The focus of PSWs' intervention is shifting towards (i) integration of the social work functions with the core functions of the organization on the one hand and (ii) of distinction of basic and allied social work functions on ground of being academic, arbitrary and fictitious on the other. PSWs accepted that: social work teaches the principle of controlled emotional involvement that helps in dealing with human beings.

In the post-globalization period, social work profession is responding to issues at the micro and macro levels; it has equal priority for interpersonal, intrapersonal concerns, special groups and community problems.

Acknowledgements

I thank God for having blessed me with this academic pursuit. Earlier, the corporate sector had kept me enchanted and I never had Ph.D. in my mind. If not for the Almighty's kindness I would have never entered academics, never pursued doctoral degree and may be would have continued to work in my hometown. I express my gratitude to Him for unveiling to me a new world of opportunities and learning.

I thank Dr. J. Christopher Daniel, (former) Faculty of Madurai Institute of Social Sciences, Madurai, Tamil Nadu. As my teacher in MSW days, Dr. Daniel ("Boss" as we fondly addressed him) sowed the seeds of professionalism in me, and also stressed on the importance of treading into hitherto unexplored areas of academic research. This work is a small way of expressing my gratitude to my mentor Dr. J. Christopher Daniel.

I am deeply indebted to Prof. (Dr.) Sanjai Bhatt, my supervisor. He had been a source of inspiration and encouragement in every stage of my work. I distinctly recall my travelling phase (for data collection) in particular – whenever I used to feel diffident, I used to draw strength from his dedication and passion for work. But for his keen interest, expert advice and constructive criticism, this study would not have been carried out successfully. I take this opportunity to thank Prof. (Dr.) Sanjai Bhatt for his guidance.

I earnestly thank all my respondents, officials of the Tata Group, who were very patient and accommodative and who amidst their heavy workload extended their co-operation.

My special thanks are to Mr. Satish Pradhan, Executive Vice President, (Group HR), Mr. Doongaji, (M D, Tata Services Limited), Mr. Anant G. Nadkarni (General Manager, Group CSR), Mr. V. K. Verma, (Head, Corporate HR, Tata Motors Limited), Mr. M.B. Paralkar, (HR Head, Tata Motors Limited, Pune), Mr. G. Ramdoss, (HR Head, Titan Industries Limited, Hosur), Mr. Niroop Mohanty, (HR Head, Tata Steel Limited, Jamshedpur), Mr. Pratap Ramdas, (IR Head, Tata Tea Limited, Munnar), Ms. Chanda Hate, (HR Head, Tata Infotech Limited, Mumbai) and Dr. Tarpada Dash (HR Head, Tata Refractories Limited, Orissa) for all their encouragement. I am grateful to Dr. S.N. Pandey, former Executive Director, Tata Steel Limited, for his help and support in approaching Tatas.

I thank the University Grants Commission, for their monetary support to this doctoral work and for partly bearing my financial burden in completing it.

I thank my parents, for all that they have done for me, for all their unsaid sacrifices which I had taken for granted. I thank my loving siblings who bore the brunt of my research blues. I thank all my friends who stood by me during those challenging years. My heartfelt thanks are due to Archana, Beena and Reji for their care and motivation. My special thanks are due to Dr. Manoj K. Jha, Associate Professor, Department of Social Work, Delhi University for being thoughtful and considerate towards my sporadic cheerlessness. I thank my husband Mr. Binay Thakur for inspiring me to publish my doctoral work.

I take this opportunity to thank all those creative minds and helpful hearts for their assistance in completing this study.

R. Nalini

Contents

LIST OF TABLES

LIST OF FIGURES

1

Social Work Practice in the Workplace : An Overview

1.1 Introduction

An overview of social work practice in industrial organizations in India and other industrialized countries has been presented in this chapter. In the backdrop of work and workplace, the human factor in workplace and the changing profile of industrial workforce, the growth and development of social work practice in industrial setting in Indian context has been discussed.

1.2. Work and Workplace

An individual spends major part of his life at work. One part of his life is spent in planning and preparing for a career that ultimately leads to work life.

Googins (1975) says :

> Work is a powerful force in our lives. It is one of man's strongest ties to reality. Most adults spend more time at work and to work-related activities than they do

> on any other activity, including sleep. It is work, for example, that meets the basic need of economic survival as well as other human needs such as satisfaction, social status, and emotional security. Work is such an overwhelming factor that most people still organize their lives around the struggle to make a living. Where we live, how we live and whom we see socially are to a great extent dominated by the work we do. (p. 464)

Workplace characteristics differ based on the type of the organization – industry development organization, education centre and so on. An industry, represents a well-defined structure in terms of duties, role expectations, flow of authority and accountability. It has a common goal – production or service delivery which it seeks to achieve through its resources – people, infrastructure, capital etc.

Nadkarni (1998) points out:

> Industry may be defined as the invention and use of tools, in order to achieve material ends. As Karl Marx put it, 'technology discloses man's mode of dealing with nature, the process of production by which he sustains life'. Industry is therefore, both an inseparable part, as well as a creation of human beings. Beginning with simple tools like bow and arrow, or the hoe or the crowbar, industry became more and more complex as human needs grew, and these simple tools were transformed gradually into more and more sophisticated machinery. (p. 1)

In the Indian context, workplace also has a social purpose. Vaid remarked that "industry in India is not only an economic organ of the society but has a social purpose as well... this social purpose is partly a derivative of social cultural forces and partly assigned to it by the state" (Vaid, 1963:134). Therefore, the nature of an workplace includes a well laid out hierarchy that clearly defines the roles and duties of individuals occupying various positions. Since the prime objective of the industrial workplace is profit making, its nature is by and large formal. Despite its formal character, some informal structures and relationships do exist simultaneously. The workplace has a set of rules, policies and procedures to ensure discipline and smooth functioning. The interest of the organization is supreme to all the individuals it comprises of, as the famous saying goes, "men may come and men may go but the organization remains".

Siddiqui (2004) explains :

> Most social work practice is essentially agency sponsored. However, as already stated, the industry is typical among the agencies in which social work is practiced. The salient features of industry are that (i) it gives priority to production and profit; (ii) individuals have value only in the context of larger goal of industry which regards them mainly as a means to an end; (iii) the relationship between the industry and the worker is close as neither can exist without the other and (iv) in its organizational structure, additional components dealing with organizational factors and mental health needs of individual workers may be found. However, the activities of these professionals and para professionals are influenced by the needs of the industrial organization rather than the needs of the workers. (p. 1).

Industry has been a major employment provider to professional social workers for many years now. Industrial organizations have been considered as an important setting for social work practice with workers/employees as client.

1.3. Characteristics of Workforce in Industries

The 1991 Census has classified workers into main workers

and marginal workers. Main workers are those workers who work for 183 or more days while those who work for less than 183 days are defined as marginal workers. Accordingly, 285.9 million (91 per cent of the total workforce) are main workers and 28.2 million (about 9 per cent) are marginal workers. About 79 per cent of the workforce resides in rural areas. Among the main workers the proportion of rural workers was about 78 per cent and that of urban workers was 22.2 per cent. On the other hand, 95 per cent of the marginal workforce was in rural areas. Another aspect of Indian workforce is its classification into organized/formal and unorganized/informal sectors. By 1994, only 8 per cent of the total workforce constituted part of the organized sector whereas the unorganized sector accounted for 92 per cent. Agriculture and allied occupations is the single largest employment provider to the Indian workforce, about 99.2 per cent of which are in the unorganized sector. In the manufacturing sector also the workers in the unorganized sector account for almost 75 per cent of the workforce. Similarly, 98 per cent of the workers in trade and commerce belong to the unorganized sector.

Dias (2003) highlights

> The growth of the labour force, employment and unemployment during 1983-2000 observed was as under:

Table 1.1 : Growth of Population, Labour Force, Employment and Unemployment

Growth Rate (%)	*1983-94*	*1994-2000*
Population	2.12	1.93
Labour Force	2.05	1.03
Employment	2.04	0.98
Organized sector employment	1.20	0.53
(a) Public	1.52	-0.03
(b) Private	0.45	1.87

> The salient points of the employment and unemployment scenario are that the rate of growth of employment declined sharply from 2.04 per cent per year in the period 1983-94 to only 0.98 per cent per year in the period 1994 to 2000.There was sharp deceleration in the growth of labour force from 2.05 per cent in the period 1983-94 to only 1.03 per cent in the period 1994-2000. Growth rate of employment is less than the growth rate of the labour force indicating an increase in the unemployment rate. The open unemployment which is of the order of 9 million is not significant compared to the size of the population in the country. Though, open unemployment is only 2.23 per cent (9 million) the percentage of the population below the poverty line is as high as 26.1 per cent. Organized sector employment is not growing and its share is only 7 per cent of the total employment. There was decline in self-employment whereas regular salaried and casual employment showed an increasing trend during 1993-94 to 1999-2000. (p. 131).

Qualitatively, there is major difference between the characteristics of workforce of yesteryears and the workers of the present period of post globalization. Agriculture was the major source of employment and income in the olden days. Alternatively, small-scale industries and handicrafts were providing earnings to the working population of the country. However, with the swiftly increasing population, there were too many hands to work – the supply of labour exceeded demand. This led to poverty and indebtedness and landless labourers migrating to industrial towns and cities for their bread and butter. The average worker was unskilled, illiterate and totally alien to the concept of an organized workplace (industry) and non-rural life. But the dismal situation of unemployment and poverty, the need to support not only himself but also his family forced him to migrate. Thus the worker in the earlier days was economically backward and psychologically under fear of the unknown.

As explained in Labour in India (1947):

> With the gradual decline and ruin of Indian handicrafts and rapid increase of population, industries on a small scale could not provide adequate and regular employment to the growing landless class. From 1870 onwards large-scale factory industries drew an increasingly large number of village workers to the cities and towns. The tremendous pressure on land in certain parts of the country assures a plentiful supply of migrant workers from the villages and prevents any considerable rise in the industrial wages. (p. 10).

The worker of the earlier days was rarely comfortable with his work front and looked for opportunities to get back to his village. Every occasion – marriage, harvest seasons, festivals became reasons for the workers to evade work. This had an effect on the workplace in the form of absenteeism and reduced production. Moreover, "often the workers have to work for long hours under unhealthy surroundings and have no means to remove the drudgery of their lives. Removed from the village community and involuntarily thrown into a strange world of the urban areas and uncongenial environment, they are liable to fall easy victims to alcoholic drinks, drugs, gambling and other such demoralizing ruinous practices and habits" (Rawat, 1988, p. 13).

The workers in workplace are in transition. The prevailing conditions have led to development of dual labour market situations. The workers in the organized sector are increasingly protected through coverage by the labour laws, although they account for no more than 8 per cent of the workforce. They are better protected by law with the collective bargaining ensured by trade union guaranteeing them the much-needed stability in work and income. Incidentally, the majority of the workforce is employed in the government owned establishments.

Bhatt (1991) has described the growth of new unionism:

> This new unionism or violent unionism is not any sudden growth, outburst or development but is a consequence of fast eroding moral social values and work ethics on one hand and growing economism on the other. Another important reason is changes in social composition of workforce and growing 'right-based awareness' among young workers. The absence of duty consciousness, revolt against 'bossism' or managerial authority, emergence of leadership from rank and file especially, young educated, lower caste urbanite or upper caste urbanite are very significant notable changes in the past three decades. (p. 13).

A number of other studies have drawn conclusions that the post- liberalization economic growth in India has not been accompanied by growth in employment. The decade (1991-2000) had, in fact experienced a "jobless growth" (Pravin, 2003).

1.4. The Human Factor in the Workplace

In the second decade of twentieth century, there were two remarkable developments – organized trade unionism and acceptance of human factor in workplace as a result of the Hawthorne experiments.

Robbins & Sanghi (2005) elaborate:

> Originally initiated by Western Electric officials and later overseen by Harvard Professor Elton Mayo, the Hawthorne Studies concluded that a worker's behaviour and sentiments were closely related; group influences were significant in affecting individual behaviour; group standards were highly effective in establishing individual worker output, and that money was less a factor in determining worker output than were group standards, sentiments, and security.

> The most important finding coming out of this study was that employees did not individually maximize their outputs. Rather, their output became controlled by a group norm that determined what a proper day's work was. So the group established its idea of a fair output – neither too much nor too little. They helped each other to ensure their reports were nearly level. (p. 235).

The upsurge of labour unions and strikes as their weapon brought into picture the workers' power. Realizing that unity was the key to most of their problems, the workers began organizing themselves. This gave them necessary strength to voice their rights and place their demands to the employers.

Described in Labour in India (1947):

> World War I not only brought huge profits to the industrialists but also led to a sharp increase in prices. Consequently, workers generated a serious strike wave in 1918-19, demanding hike in wages to match correspondingly increasing market prices. The initial success of some strikes not only promoted solidarity among the workers but also attracted leaders and organizers from the intelligentsia into the labour movement. The non-cooperation movement launched by Mahatma Gandhi in 1919-21 had a profound effect on the masses as well as on workers who realized their important role in the economy of the country. These conditions led to the formation of a large number of trade unions. The year 1920 saw the establishment of Textile Labour Association at Ahmedabad. In 1921 Mr. N.M. Joshi introduced a trade union bill, which after five years of persistent effort – saw the light as the Indian Trade Union Act, 1926. (p. 45).

The government machinery geared into action to protect

the workers who with all their inadequacies such as illiteracy, economic backwardness, and alienation were vulnerable to exploitation. It appointed various committees to look into conditions of workers at the factories and to understand their needs and problems. The next step was enacting appropriate labour laws thereby statutorily regulating working conditions in favour of the workers and strengthening their bargaining power with the employers.

Soon, the human factor in the workplace – more specifically human relations in industrial organizations became the buzzword and panacea to all ills and problems in workplace. It also became the prime concern of social work profession on its inception. Explaining the importance of human factor in the workplace, McGregor (1960) emphatically made a point that:

> The intellectual potentials of the average human being are only partially utilized under the conditions of modern industrial life. The limits on human collaboration in the organizational setting are not limits of human nature but of management's ingenuity in discovering how to realize the potential represented by its human resources. Management cannot provide a man with self-respect, or with the respect of his fellows or with the satisfaction of needs for self-fulfilment. We can create conditions such that he is encouraged and enabled to seek such satisfactions for himself, or we can thwart him by failing to create these conditions. (p. 41).

Workers/employees, who offer their services in return for wages or salary, are definitely major stakeholders in operations, if not in ownership. Akbas (1979) mentioned that social work in workplace deals with the adjustment of the workers of all levels to their work, to the enterprise, to their colleagues, chiefs and subordinates as well as with the adaptation of work and working situation to the human being. Its efforts contribute simultaneously to human well-being and to greater efficiency. Increased concern for the quality of life at the worksite and beyond has been a prime motivating factor behind the social work programmes in industrial settings. It places the human being in the centre, whereas the total organization is directed to the work that must be performed. The consequence of this approach is that the social worker can give full attention to his client, while the line executives have to divert their attention amongst a great number of subjects of which the worker is only one.

The aim of social work has been to bring about optimum adaptation of the individual with his or her environment thereby augmenting social functioning.

Upadhyay (2003) remarks:

> Boehm (1958) noted that social work seeks to enhance the social functioning of individuals, singly and in groups by activities focused upon their social relationships which constitute the interaction between man and his environment. These activities can be grouped into three functions: restoration of impaired capacity, provision of individual and social resources, and prevention of social dysfunction. Every member of the society continues to function in some role or the other and any obstacle to role performance by the individual creates a problem to social functioning. How and with what effectiveness an individual performs his various roles is the main focus of the social work intervention. (p.3).

From the social work point of view, "the exclusion of the work experience, in its fuller meaning, suggests a vast unused source of data and resources that may be helpful in intervention process" (Vigilante, 1993, p. 182).

Some benevolent employers introduced welfare measures voluntarily in a gradual manner. Majority of the employers, nevertheless, followed the statutory regulations imposed upon them by the government. Social work profession found a firm footing in the workplace with the introduction of the Factories Act, 1948. The labour welfare officer was expected to play the social worker in workplace. He had a whole array of functions all aiming to provide labour welfare, promote harmonious industrial relations, and ultimately bring about the person-environment adaptation. With his position being statutorily guarded, the labour welfare officer was here to stay. Above all, the development had been regarded as a step forward to place human factor above other three Ms- machine, material and money.

1.5. Changing Scenario: Changing Needs

With history of more than one century of unionization, government interventions and employers statutory and non-statutory welfare efforts, workplace and workforce both have undergone tremendous changes in its dimensions. The steady flow of fixed income enabled establishment of basic living standards for the worker and his family. From individual worker to his family, education and awareness brought lot many changes, in the qualitative and quantitative workforce. A beginning was made in education of the workers' families. Ruralite, illiterate, unskilled and manual workers are replaced by urbanite, educated, skilled and technology friendly workforce in large and medium industries. Migration and its related problems were slowly getting reduced. As Datt & Sundaram (2005, p. 721) observe, "Only in recent years, a new class of industrial labour without roots in agriculture is emerging in our towns and cities". This trend was evident till the 1990s, the pre-liberalization era. However, after Liberalization, Privatization and Globalization (LPG) the workforce is characterized by changes in past few years. The attitude and expectations of the workforce towards the organization and *vice versa* also underwent a change. While *sons of the soil or life time employment* was an essential aspect of earlier workforce, now employability' of the workforce within and outside his organization is becoming more important. Widespread technological revolution shrinking the globe as village has definitely increased access to information and awareness of the average worker. This has been matched by the change in the nature of work due to thrust on automation and also because of inclusion of new sectors. For example, industries include service and hospitality sectors that demanded a different profile of the human resource to be employed. The need of the hour was a more educated, young and aware workforce. This workforce had begun to accommodate women in increasing numbers thus fostering shift in gender roles. Against this background of series of fast changes occurring in the workforce and in workplace, the needs and problems of the workforce have also witnessed dramatic changes.

The workplace is a reflection of the larger society. The problems beset in the society are likely to be present in the workplace too, due to the human element common to both.

According to Datt & Sundaram (2005):

> Industrial labour in India is not united, but is divided and sub-divided on the basis of region, religion, language and caste. It is only in recent years that some of these difficulties are disappearing gradually and some degree of unity on the basis of economic consideration is taking place (p. 721).

"In the absence of social insurance and unemployment benefits there is a widespread concern about the negative fall outs of the thin organized sector employment becoming thinner. There is increasing contractualization and casualisation and a large scale retrenchment. (Mishra, 2001, p. 14). The workers need to be provided with alternatives to deal with such a situation, considering their skills and demands of the changing job market. The functioning of the workplace is also undergoing change that may have an undesired effect on the worker. "Changes in workplace are taking place through reduction in the levels of labour hierarchy, job classifications, introduction of multi-task, multi-skilled work system and making a significant portion (25 per cent to over 50 per cent of cost isolated cases) of pay as variable pay depending on performance" (Mishra, 2001, p. 14).

The needs of the labour market have undergone a sea change. Job security may soon be a thing of the past, since part-time or specific project based employment is rampant. Trade Unions are slowly losing their strength and as a result, its bargaining power. Many reasons could be attributed to this such as : "high and rising levels of unemployment and severe underemployment in many parts of the world, jobless growth, large scale recession in workplace, shrinkage of jobs in the organized sector, increase in rationalization, retrenchment, closure and resultant displacement of labour in the organized sector on the one hand and rapid growth of the informal sector on the other" (Mishra, 2001, p.23). Such a situation calls for concerted efforts from all concerned to bring about a balanced growth of the workplace and its people. Since this new situation requires positive interventions from most of the human service professions, social work profession has a major role to play at this crucial juncture.

Social Work and the Workplace: An Overview

In India, labour welfare has been one of the major areas of social work practice since the beginning of social work education and training. The need for welfare services grew with gradual growth of industrialization and it was shaped by different factors and forces affecting the organizational structure, quantitative and qualitative changes in the workforce, degree of unionization, state intervention and regulation and development of management sciences. The Royal Commission of Labour in 1931 recommended the appointment of welfare officers to deal with the problems of workforce and to settle their grievances at workplace. Thus specialized education and training in social work for preparing welfare personnel for the labour field started in 1936. In 1948, it received legal recognition and about a dozen schools of social work came forward to train the manpower required to manage welfare services in workplace. During the decade of 1950-60, industrial organizations faced problems of industrial relations, which necessitated personnel to maintain harmonious industrial relations in the organizations. Since welfare officers were executing it as part of their duties, many social work professionals shifted to this new position. They had an edge over other management graduates because of their unique training in human relations in general and social work methods (especially casework and group work) in particular. Following demands from the field, management schools started courses in industrial relations and personnel management. Soon management graduates (with degree in business administration) also started taking up positions of personnel/industrial relations officers in industrial organizations. However many social work graduates continued shifting to industrial relations/ personnel officer posts. This trend was also influenced by employers' individual attitude towards managing industrial relations and welfare programmes. Simultaneously, the need for counselling services made employee assistance programmes grow in the West. The growing number of alcoholic employees created the demand for social workers in industries. In India, some progressive employers like the Tata and Godrej appointed counsellors, whereas others have delegated this responsibility to the welfare officers. As a result three major areas of social work practice emerged in workplace namely Labour Welfare (LW), Industrial Relations

(IR) and Personnel Administration (PA) and some organizations brought them under the department of Personnel Management (PM).

Workplace has been a major employment provider to professional social workers for many years now. Industrial organizations have been considered as an important setting for social work practice with workers/employees. Tata Group has pioneered social work interventions in the field of labour welfare in India. The first full time welfare officer of the country was in Empress Mills, Nagpur where the welfare officer successfully developed a number of activities. These include refreshment shops in Mills, meal sheds, co-operative stores, a co-operative credit society, maternity benefits, crèches, a boy scouts organization, recreations and amusements of different kinds and an extensive educational scheme (Report of the Royal Commission on Labour in India, 1931). The founder of Tata Steel, J.N.Tata, believed that what comes from the people must be returned to the people – that the wealth generated by any workplace must be used to benefit the people to enrich their lives. The well-being of their employees has been a concern of Tata organizations. Tata Steel has been a pioneer in introducing many firsts in the area of employee welfare, industrial counselling, employee assistance programme, corporate social responsibility, social auditing etc. Some of the welfare firsts of Tata Steel such as eight hour working day, free medical aid, establishment of the welfare department, leave with pay, workers' PF scheme, workmen's accident compensation scheme, and maternity scheme etc., introduced as early as 1912 became rationales to enact legislative protection by National and State Governments. As years passed by the Tatas commitment to welfare grew beyond its employees to society at large. Tata Steel instituted an independent social audit to evaluate how far the company has been able to fulfil its social and moral responsibilities. In 1980 the report of the social audit committee stated that "we are satisfied that the social performance of the Company is of high order and its magnitude, is perhaps unequalled in India" (Monappa, 1997: 254). The Tatas have attempted innovative measures and set trends in various aspects of employee well-being, irrespective of industries in its umbrella – plantations, engineering, automobiles, information technology, electronics etc. As known to all, Tata has also pioneered education and training in social work by establishing the Sir Dorabji Graduate School of Social Work which was later renamed as the Tata Institute of Social Sciences.

The first school of social work in India, Sir Dorabji Graduate School of Social Work that was renamed as Tata Institute of Social Sciences in 1944 also felt the need of starting a full-fledged two-year course in Personnel Management and Industrial Relations in 1967.

Singh (2005) observed:

> In 1948, the Factories Act was enacted in which specific provision was made under section 49 for the appointment of Labour Welfare Officers whose qualifications were also laid down under the relevant rules, which incorporated, *inter alia,* Master's degree in Social Work with specialization in labour welfare and industrial relations as minimum qualification for appointment to this post. Though specialization oriented social work has continued to exist mainly because of availability of employment opportunities in diverse fields, yet it has been a subject of debate throughout, leading to division among social work educators, which became so sharp that there was voting among social work educators who were participating in Udaipur Seminar in 1982, and the overwhelming majority decision was that specialization would continue as a part of the social work curriculum (p. 18).

Later, the human resources development approach,

which was more akin to social work philosophy and values broadened the scope of social work practice in industries. This new HRD approach focused on investment in employees, productivity improvement through skill building, welfare beyond the boundaries of workplace, taking care of inter and intra personal problems of workforce and inclusion of corporate social responsibilities. This forced many social work departments such as Lucknow, Baroda, Jamia and Agra, to start specialized courses in Human Resources Management and Human Resource Development. "Social work practice promotes human well-being by strengthening opportunities, resources and capacities of people in their environments and by creating policies and services to correct conditions that limit human rights and quality of life" (Mohan, 2003: 113). The social work professionals in industrial organizations are engaged in varied positions performing different kinds of functions ranging from labour welfare, employee relations, personnel administration, employee counselling, community development, employee assistance and corporate social responsibility. However the issue of desirability of social work practice in industrial setting is still a matter of debate.

Social work professionals in Indian industries appear to be in various fields involving the development and management of human resources, labour welfare, industrial relations, community welfare, CSR etc. Considering the changes in their roles, functions and positions especially in post-globalization period, the study intended to explore varied kinds of practices by social work professionals in industrial organizations. The study has attempted to examine social work practices in select industrial organizations of the Tata Group.

2

Social Work in the Indian Workplace

2.1 Historical Perspective of Social Work in the Indian Workplace

The concern area for the social worker has been the human component in the workplace. Workplace is a microscopic India, fetching diversity in all aspects.

In the words of Desai & Dole (1979):

> The entry point of social work in industry was sometimes the family planning programmes. However, it has been noticed that once the social worker is appointed her functions broaden to several areas of preventive and curative services with the employees. In 1964 the Tata Institute of Social Sciences undertook a pilot project of industrial social work at the request of a private tobacco company. The major emphasis was on handling problems of absenteeism, indebtedness and work adjustments. Subsequently, the worker was absorbed in the industry as an employee counselling officer. (p. 16).

The genesis and growth of the social work practice *vis a vis* the profession in workplace is traced briefly and categorized in five phases on the basis of its characteristics.

2.1.1. Initiation Phase: Prior to 1936

Prior to 1936, social work in workplace could be characterized as *initiation* phase as there were many individual initiatives with different motives – predominantly philanthropic in approach. This period was marked by voluntary efforts of progressive employers towards welfare of their workers.

As per Kumar (1992) quoted in Bhatt (2001):

> Even before the legislative provisions for appointment of welfare officers were brought, some employers and associations like the Bombay Mills Owners Association, Indian Jute Mill Association appointed Labour or Welfare Officer to look after labour related matters in the decade thirties. Even in the year 1923, Tata Steel had appointed Mr. K.A. Naroji as welfare officer. Royal Commission recommended employment of labour officers in factories. In 1931, the institutionalization of welfare officer in India had three peculiar features: (i) protection of job by government, (ii) the neutral position in all disputes between employers and employees and (iii) multi-purpose officer. Despite all such efforts, this institution constantly remained under criticism and neglected by all. (p. 37).

As it is evident, even during those years of exploitation of labour, some progressive-minded employers had made beginnings that could be termed as social work practice. Emergence of trade unions also contributed to growth of labour welfare.

Sati (1972) observed:

> During this period there was serious industrial unrest. It was in this period that workers united themselves through Trade Unions. For the first time the then government took the step for safeguarding the interests of the workers through the enactment of the

> Indian Trade Union Act of 1926, to prevent the exploitation by the employers and ensuring the employees protection even when they took part in trade union work and the Trade Dispute Act also made provisions for constituting bodies for investigation and settlement of disputes. (p. 7).

Then there were a series of protective legislations for working class with the much needed legal support to fight against their exploitation by the employers.

Siddiqui & Sukhramani (2001) find:

> All these developments apart from being instrumental in the promulgation of labour legislation such as the Indian Mines Act, 1923, Workmen's Compensation Act, 1923, Maternity Benefit Acts (separate acts in each of the provinces) Indian Factories (Amendment Act, 1922) influenced the appointment of Royal Commission on Labour in 1929. The Royal Commission on Labour was set up to enquire into and report on the then existing conditions of labour in industrial undertakings, plantations, etc., in British India. The Commission made an in-depth survey of different aspects of health, efficiency, welfare, standard of living, and conditions of work etc. (Sharma, 1993). Most of the suggestions made by the Commission found approval with the government and were implemented. The Commission can also be seen as the stimulus for the introduction of labour welfare officers in industrial organizations. (p. 45).

Though the initiation phase began with philanthropic mindsets it nevertheless paved the way for protective approach towards workforce.

2.1.2. Integration Phase: From 1936 to 1952

During this period the need for professional services to

manage workers' problems at workplace was recognized and included in policy to handle workers' needs and problems. Social work was marked by interest of political leaders in uniting the struggling workers and also the advent of professional social work in India. "The Labour Investigation Committee (Rege Committee) of 1944-46 studied the living and working conditions of labour in different industries and Bhor Committee on Health and Social Security had become milestone in the development of labour welfarism" (Bhatt, 2001, p. 36). The beginning for professional social work education was made in the year 1936 by the Tatas.

Kudchedkar (1966) illustrates:

> The year 1936 is considered important in the history of social work education in India because of establishment of the Sir Dorabji Tata Graduate School of Social Work by the Sir Dorabji Tata Trust in Bombay as the first post-graduate institution for the training of professional social workers against the background of the long and rich tradition of voluntary social service in the country. The school imparted a 2 years' generic course in professional social work under the direction of Dr.Clifford Manshardt, an American Missionary, who was also in charge of the *Nagpada Neighbourhood House* of the American Marathi Mission. The School of Social Work was renamed to Tata Institute of Social Sciences in 1944 which introduced two and half years' specialization course in different fields of social work such as (i) Family and Child Welfare, (ii) Medical and Psychiatric Social Work, and (iii) Labour Welfare, Industrial Relations and Personnel Management in 1947. (p. 1).

The government and managements paved the path for social work interventions through formal and informal ways. Since government machinery was geared into action immediately after Independence to meet out problems of an emerging nation, much protective and promotive legislation was brought into force. In 1948, through the Factories Act, it introduced measures to ensure health, safety and welfare that had to be implemented by employers compulsorily. Section 49 of the Act brought forth the appointment of welfare officers (in a factory where 500 or more workers are employed). The Act further specified qualifications of the welfare officer that included professional social work degree. In a bid to make their role effective, the Act also stipulated that the respective State Government lay down (Factories) Rules on the procedure to be followed in appointment of these welfare officers. With this statutory requirement, the entry of professional social workers in workplace gained a fresh impetus. The labour welfare officer was here to stay, as he had become a legal requirement.

In the words of Bhatt (2001):

> Finally, the state wedded to the idea of "welfare state" and commitment towards welfare found adequate space in the Indian Constitution in 1950. Despite much talks of welfare, everyone i.e., employers, government and unions could not translate the concepts and spirit of welfare into their programmes and actions. With respect to developing implementation agencies for welfare, the setting up Labour Officers pool came in action during the Second World War. Later on, the government has statutorily created the institution of Welfare Officers under section 49 of the Factories Act, 1948. It was provided that: (i) in every factory wherein five hundred or more workers are ordinarily employed, the employer shall employ in the factory such number of welfare officers as may be prescribed, (ii) the State Government may prescribe the duties, qualification and conditions of service of such officers employed. Similar provisions were made for plantations and the mines workers under the Plantation Labour Act, 1951 and Mines Act, 1952. (p. 36).

From the duties of the welfare officer it emerged that he was to play an increasingly advisory role, building bridges of harmonious employer-employee relations.

As quoted by Sati (1972):

> The statutory duties call upon him to act as welfare services manager, and as a 'staff' functionary in matters of personnel management and labour relations all at the same time and within the same setting. In the discharge of his duties the labour welfare officer must act as a "neutral" functionary, a sort of buffer, between management and labour. (p. 8).

In brief, this phase has been titled as inclusion since one finds that workers have received priority in various spheres of industrial organization at various levels. The state intervention moved from legislative protection to problem solving of workers at individual, group and community level as various mechanisms and agencies were geared towards workers welfare. Social work schools recognized workplace as one of the emerging field of intervention as well as a major employment provider.

2.1.3. Inclusion Phase: From 1952 to 1975

This period has been called inclusion phase because it was marked by inclusion of various approaches, efforts and measures towards welfare of workers. There has been frequent disruption of work activities, worse industrial relations, intense trade unionism, innovation in services for workers etc. on the one hand with various stakeholders showing positive shift from protective approach to problem solving outlook on the other. There was increased emphasis on maintaining harmonious industrial relations, response to individual and group problems, attention on personal care and family welfare, profit sharing mechanisms in the form of bonus, focus on personnel practices, etc. At this juncture the social workers in workplace made their presence felt in managing harmonious industrial relations and accepting challenges of personnel management. Kudchedkar (1966) pointed out the emergence of the new personnel officer in India against the historical background of the Labour Officers of the 1930s and Welfare Officers of the 1950s as a significant professional development in the world of welfare. This new functionary reflected the modern trend of the American and British industrial development after the Second World War. As a result, the labour field today has three main areas: Labour Welfare (LW), Industrial Relations (IR) and Personnel Administration (PA) that together have formed the new professional area of Personnel Management (PM) as part of the management in industry. The phenomenal rise of personnel management can be traced back to the western countries.

Described by Kudchedkar (1979):

> In the West, management as a profession was growing rapidly during the 1950s and the 1960s and the influence of this new professional discipline was inescapable in India. This was seen in the growth of two professional practitioners' associations, namely the *National Institute of Labour Management* in Bombay and the *Indian Institute of Personnel Management* in Calcutta and Bombay. Broadly, the picture of profession that has emerged in recent years covers the following professional areas: employment and manpower planning; training and development; wages and remuneration systems; health, safety and welfare benefits; communication and consultation; negotiations and disputes settlement. (p. 35-36).

Besides movement of social workers to handle the position of industrial relations officers, some of the progressive industries also appointed industrial counsellors/ employees counsellors/industrial social workers. A professional social worker's career path in workplace normally begins as Labour Welfare Officer. After some experience, they move to either the position of the Industrial Relations Officer which ends at the position of the Personnel and Administration Officer. Some social workers do occupy senior positions with their individual calibre, interest and organizational needs. However, with the opening of *para* positions for some specified tasks like counselling, family welfare, and health services came the need for social workers. Some industrial houses like Tata, Mahindra, J.K, opened family welfare and community development departments. Therefore, the need for employing a professional social worker to take care exclusively of the social work department was felt. This led to new openings in industrial social work.

During the 1960-70 decade, the Indian industries have also seen the diversification of social work positions. Personnel Social Work came as a multi-faceted perspective.

Elucidated by Kudchedkar (1979):

> Similar to the European experience, social work graduates became labour welfare officers, assistant personnel officers, personnel officers and personnel managers in industry. As a result the original objective of social workers in industry underwent a change during the 1960-70s with the advent of the management education in India. Hence, personnel social work emerged as a speciality of the social work. Unfortunately, the professional curricula in personnel management and industrial relations have not been able to place personnel social work as an independent specialization. (p. 49).

It has been also titled as industrial social work and industrial counselling but the western term *personnel social work* could not attain popularity.

2.1.4. Innovation Phase: From 1975 to 1990

The phase has been characterized as progressive and participatory. The beginning of this phase was marked by imposition of internal emergency in the country through *Defence of India Rules* and *Maintenance of Internal Security Act*. During emergency, fundamental rights including right to strike were suspended. This created a working environment without labour unrest as all trade union activities touched an all time low.

During this phase, the worker became employee and human resource. Personnel management took the form of Human Resource Management (HRM) with emphasis on individual dignity and worth. In the mid 80's, human resource management emerged on the industrial scene. Bear *et al.* (1984) have asserted that human resource management permeates all management decisions and actions, which in turn, have a bearing on the relationship between organization and its employees. A significant event, which underscored the significance of personnel management during this period, has been the merger of the Indian Institute of Personnel Management and the National Institute of Labour Management to form the National Institute of Personnel Management (Aswathappa, 2002). Soon, it took the form of Human Resource Development (HRD). The philosophy of HRD was more akin to professional social work philosophical tenets and values. Investment in employees to build their capacities became cornerstone. Employees Assistance Programme (EAP) started gaining ground as matter of result oriented employee centred programme. Corporate Social Responsibility (CSR) had an enhanced, planned and pragmatic approach in the place of philanthropic concern. Human resource management gained wide recognition as a distinct discipline and today it has become so popular that many Departments/Schools of Social Work have started separate courses in human resource management (Singh, 2004). Viswanathan (1963) expressed that the scope of social work professionals expanded to cover industrial relations and personnel management and more recently human resource management. These social workers are designated as welfare officers, industrial relations officers/managers, or personnel/human resource managers. Thus within industrial organizations, a number of trained social workers are working but into departments as diverse as labour welfare, personnel, public relations etc. These professionals were expected to perform a variety of functions (Siddiqui & Sukhramani, 2001). Professional social workers in workplace have ample scope for career advancement.

Navale & Desai (2002) said:

> Developing potentials of human beings to the maximum possible level is social work objective and social workers are trained well to achieve this objective which provides them competitive edge to function as Human Resource Developer or as Human Resource Managers. Professionally trained social workers occupy various positions right from trainee to Vice-President (H.R.) in industrial organization practice social work and they stand out with their human touch in their day-to-day functioning. (p. 2).

Bhatt (2001) has summarized the development of social work in workplace in terms of various positions, their period, major functions, organizational hierarchy and qualification for employing trained social workers in an industrial organization in tabular form which presents a bird's eye view of social work in workplace in India. Social work professionals successfully took up all these positions in an industrial organization.

Table 2.1: Various positions, their period, major functions, organizational hierarchy and qualification for employing trained social workers in an industrial organization (Bhatt, 2001: 48)

Position in Industry	*Period of Evolution*	*Nature of Work/ Major Task*	*Organizational Hierarchy*	*Requisite Qualification*
Labour Officers	1930-40	To look after labour problems especially recruitment and labour disputes; To help in retaining workers, link with jobbers	Officer reporting tofactory manager	No educational qualification was prescribed, any graduate or even an experienced person
Welfare Officer	1940-50	To maintain human relations, to administer welfare services, to help workers in their adjustment	Statutory, Mult-purpose officer, Equivalent to head of the Deptt., Part of Personnel Deptt.	Degree in Social Work with speciali-zation in labour welfare/human relations
Personnel Officer	1950-60	To manage personnel functions especially personnel admini-stration/human relations	Enjoys executive head position among other officers, line and staff functions both	Master degree in Manage-ment / social science with law as desirable qualification
Industrial Relations Officer	1960-65	To handle industrial relations/ workers' grievances, collective bar-gaining and union's resistance	Subordinate to Personnel Officer as in charge of one of the PM's function	Degree in Social Work with specialization in IRPM/LW
Employee Counselling	1965	Counselling to workers and their families	As a part of welfare function, supervisor level	Degree in Social Work/ Psychology/ Counselling
Industrial Social Work	1960-70	Personalized curative services for employees in problems (distress, work adjustment, relationship) Substance addiction	As a part of welfare function, supervisory level Degree in Social Work/	Industrial Relations & Per-sonnel Manage-ment

(Contd...)

Table 2.1: *(Contd...)*

Human Resource Management	1970-80	Enlarged personnel functions with emphasis on IR for overall development of employees with emphasis on training and development or employees as Human resources	Prominent place in the Organiza-tion	Post graduate degree/ diploma in Social Work HRM/ IRM/HRD degree in Management
Human Resource Development	1980-90	HRD, integration of all functions, Employee Assistance, Welfare, Counselling, Services, Development	Reorganization of PM/HRM units as separate Department	Welfare/MSW/MHRM/MBA/ MGORD/PG Dip HRD

2.1.5. Imitative Phase: From 1990 onwards

This period has been termed as imitative because many programmatic approaches has been imitated from western countries after globalization. The period saw the rise and growth of HRD with focus on employee development through human relations, training and employee participation. Workplace, in the era of Liberalization, Privatization and Globalization (LPG) has realized that human resources are the biggest assets of the organization.

Bhatt (2001) describes the employee development model:

> The central thesis of this model lies in the emerging philosophy of HRD considering workforce as human resource in the place of workers or employees. The model laid emphasis on independence of their contribution to corporate productivity or profit, democratic values of trust, integrity and belief in employees' potential and respect for their dignity. This creates [an] organizational climate with a sense of involvement and belongingness where people find fulfilment in work, seek newer horizon for themselves and the enterprise through self and subordinate development. The model generates services and programmes which requires training, retraining, development, participatory involvement, self-development, self-management, self-help groups, cooperative credit and thrift societies. Since programmes are unconventional, unusual, innovative, role expectations also varies. Social workers are searching newer management means and ways. Linkage of occupational health and safety with *yoga*, mediation, naturopathy, stress coping mechanism, and to personality development under welfare are signs of newer approaches. A social work

> professional has to perform role as researcher, explorer, advocate and crusader. Some schools of social work initiated need-based innovative programmes. Lucknow School of Social Work has started academic programme in Yoga and Naturopathy. The Department of Social Work, Jamia Milia Islamia has started two years course in Human Resource Management. Loyola College, Trivandrum has started a two years programme in human relations management. A number of corporate houses and non-governmental organizations have already started such programmes for their employees. Employee Assistance Programmes are a new addition. It is therefore evident that trained social work graduates are engaged in wide variety of roles as administrator, advocate, broker, counsellor, facilitator, mediator, negotiator, organizer, programme planner, resource person, supervisor, stimulator, etc. (p. 42-43).

2.2. Social Work Practice in the Workplace: Major Areas

Social work knowledge has been found useful in workplace and it may be looked at from a variety of perspectives. There are broadly two ways: (i) exclusive practice of traditional social work methods, principles and techniques with clients group and (ii) inclusive practice of social work in managing and developing of human resources of the organization through creation of an enabling environment. It also ranges from problem solving to programme management to programme development to policy formulation. The roles an individual plays at the workplace and outside work are very much under the domain of social work intervention in industry.

As Plessis (2001) reiterated:

> The concept of *"employee-as-person" vis-a-vis "person-as-employee"* – the division inherent therein corresponds well respectively with "social work in industry" and "industrial social work". In the first conceptualization the emphasis is on serving the employee in his/her non-work role – such as father, mother, brother, daughter, and community member. In the case of *"employee-as-person"* work roles become the focus of social work concern: for example, a stressed manager, sexually harassed female worker, over loaded apprentice, advancing manager, discriminated against minority group work and retrenched employee. (p. 108).

The focus here is not only reacting to problem situations but also on being proactive in preventing them.

2.2.1 Labour Welfare

In India, labour welfare has been a key area for social workers' intervention and practice. In manufacturing organizations, social workers generally begin their career as labour welfare officers. The main job responsibility of labour welfare officers is to ensure compliance of statutory requirements of welfare related to workplace, workers and their surrounding. This lead to the social workers getting involved with administrative business, organizational development, routine office management, records maintenance and working closely with government authorities.

As Rawat (1988) defines:

> Labour welfare is a part of social welfare conceptually and operationally. The total concept is a desirable state of existence involving well-being, physical, mental, moral and emotional of workers. The Labour Investigation Committee (1944-46) includes under labour welfare activities anything done for the intellectual, physical, moral and economic betterment

> of the workers and their surrounding communities whether by employers, by Government or by other agencies over and above what is laid down by law or what is normally expected as part of the contractual benefits for which the workers may have bargained. (p. 4).

2.2.2 Personnel/Human Resources Management

As HR (formerly personnel) specialists, social workers are in the mainstream of the organization and have scope for applying social work principles and methods at policy-making level. From implementers, they become decision-makers. In all HR functions – from R to R (Recruitment to Retirement) the social work orientation could be embedded. The ultimate objective of social workers in HR shall be to make the entire organization 'social work sensitive'.

Personnel management and social work have much in common. As defined by Breach, "personnel management is that part of management's process which is primarily concerned with the human constitutents of an organization", Edison defines "personnel management is the service of human engineering" (Sharma, 1997, p. 83).

Vaid (1963) lists out:

> Thus, personnel management has three objectives. It must contribute to the effective functioning of the business; it must help the human factor to grow and develop (which is possible only by making work satisfying to them) and it must fulfil the social and societal obligations of the industry. (p. 134).

Human resource management, the new form of personnel management, considered employees as human capital and assets to the organization. The Human Resource Development (HRD) emphasized on motivating employees for their own development and empowerment. "The social worker as a human resource specialist represents a hybrid of social worker and personnel specialist, who is beginning to affect the direction and contours of the work environment" (Googins & Godfrey 1987, p.10).

2.2.3. Counselling

Counselling is one of the key job responsibilities of a social worker in industry. While one finds industrial social workers or EAP professional appointed exclusively for employee counselling, experience indicates that almost all social workers utilize counselling as a technique in executing their duties. These sessions are not structured or do not fulfil the documentation criteria to be called counselling in the strictest sense. Yet, the counselling process takes place consistently.

"Counselling is a process which takes place on a one-to-one relationship between an individual troubled by a problem with which he cannot cope himself and a professional whose training and experience helps the other reach solutions to various types of personal difficulties" (Gajendragad, 2004, p.1).

2.2.4. Occupational/Industrial Social Work

"The term 'occupational social work' is not one that is commonly used in the United Kingdom or Ireland, though it is to be found in use in the United States and some other countries. It refers to the application of social work knowledge, skills and values to the workplace problems. This is not simply 'welfare work' as used in many companies and organizations. It is a lot more than that". *(www.avenueconsulting.co.uk)*

Every organization's industrial social work practices are need-specific. It springs out of a situation in which the problem to be tackled is more psychological in nature. For instance, in an organization the need was felt because of the diversity in cultures of its employees. It consisted of employees from different social, economic, linguistic, educational and cultural backgrounds. Many employees were from states other than the one where the organization was located resulting in culture shock, language barrier and poor social support. The employees were young, mostly unmarried and prone for adjustment problems. Apart from linguistic bias and administrative problems the point of serious concern was the insecurity in the minds of the employees. The industrial social worker was appointed primarily to turn these threats into opportunities for growth.

Wyers & Kaulukukui (1984) explain:

> Ozawa outlines a four-stage process of industrial social service department. Stage 1 is the conventional provision of social services dealing with specific personal problems. In stage 2, a comprehensive programme evolves with a wide range of activities, which may include consultation, a variety of educational programes, and recreational activities. Stage 3 shifts the focus from the individual worker alone to organizational intervention. Stage 4 is characterized by management and employees working together in developing a sense of community within the organization. The majority of programes have not developed beyond Stage 2. (p. 167)

2.2.5. Employee Assistance Programmes

Employee Assistance Programmes (EAP) is one of the latest forms of social work practice in industry.

Googins & Godfrey, 1987 define:

> EAP is a system for identifying and treating a variety of medical or behavioural problems that might be responsible for employee's poor job performance. Its

> main objective is to restore an employee to normal work behaviour and productivity.

The major assumptions underlying EAP are as follows:

1. Unless job performance is impaired, person's life or problem is his own.
2. Most problems, regardless of their nature, eventually manifest themselves in poor performance.
3. It is the role of the supervisors to measure and evaluate job performance. Thus they can identify deteriorating job performance without having to diagnose the nature of the underlying problem (p. 102).

EAP in India is in its formative stages with few multinational organizations implementing it in their organizations.

2.2.6. Corporate Social Responsibility

One of the upcoming trends of social work in workplace is corporate social responsibility.

Pandey (1991) says:

> The Business owes its responsibilities towards society; first, as a result of the impact of its own operations and secondly, as the unit of the society in which it operates. The former is related to what the organization does to society by way of its specific operations, whereas the latter deals with what the society demands from it. Nevertheless, regardless of reasons, business organizations need to discharge social responsibilities, even though they may not be directly responsible for social problems. (p. 12).

Anthony (1984) finds:

> 'There is a most intimate connection between decency and good business', as Ford put it (1922:100). Ford, however, extended the notion of service to a second level in which the business institution can be expected to take on wide community responsibilities, 'everyone who is connected with us, either as a manager, worker or purchaser – is the better for our existence. The institution which we have erected is performing a service' (1922:19). This meant, said Ford that factories should be cross-sections of the community and should employ a due proportion of disabled people.

It is found that many organizations and business groups are including social responsibility in their initiatives and are increasingly appointed qualified social workers for its execution.

2.3. Roles of a social worker in the Workplace

The diverse roles a social worker plays in the workplace help them understand social work and company objectives in a neutral manner. The roles adorned by social workers in an industrial organization are given below:

- Employee Welfare Officer
- Industrial Relations Officer
- Human Resources/Personnel Officer
- Community Development Officer
- Industrial Social Worker
- Counsellor

Working for a profit making organization requires social workers to make decisions that are influenced by financial imperatives.

As explained by Googins & Godfrey (1987):

- To the workplace and these multitudinous roles social workers bring core social work concepts and skills;
- A psychosocial understanding of individuals in relation to the environment.
- Relationship building and contract establishment
- Use of the self as a tool
- An ability to listen with the "third ear" (i.e. well developed diagnostic and assessment skills). (p. 10).

2.4. Social Work in the Workplace: The Debate in India

While it is evident that workplace requires the services of the social workers, it is also true that there is mutual hesitation in accepting this fact. Social work in workplace has been viewed more often with resentment than receptivity.

Elaborated by Siddiqui & Sukhramani (2001):

> Social work in the workplace has generated a lot of debate among social workers in India. Conceptually, the scope of such work is seen to include counselling, organization of support groups, concrete services, linking the individual to community services, training and staff development, and providing consultation to workers and management within the context of large scale industrial or other commercial organizations. The activities a social worker is expected to perform in meeting workers' needs and in particular development needs and combining it with the broader organizational goals generate tension, which is inevitable. The employee welfare and development and corporate profits are two ends of a continuum and may often be difficult to reconcile within a philosophical perspective. It becomes all the more problematic in view of the professional commitment of the worker to the values of social

> justice. The social worker thus may have to make a conscious choice of being pro-management or pro-worker, though his/her activities may be the same. This has led to a debate among social work educators, in allowing industrial houses to become a major consumer of the products of social work departments. (p. 1).

N. Vishwanathan, as early as 1963 questioned:

> The question of whether there is a place for social work in industry is not simply answered. It seems there are at least two opposing ideological standpoints, which are prevalent. On the one hand, there are some social work educators and practitioners who maintain that industrial social work is farce. The value orientation of social work is that the resources of the society must be used to bring maximum opportunities of the individual, whereas that of industry is primarily profit and hence the values of social work and industry are incompatible. On the other hand, there are those who feel that there need not be any inherent contradictions or conflicts in the goals of the industry. Social work and industry are both institutions of society. They derive support from each other. The emerging concept of social work in industry refers to the reciprocity of objectives. (p. 63)

Isn't it strange that even decades after, the status and views of social work in workplace remains almost the same? This, despite the fact that the inflow of social work professionals to the workplace has been continuing over these years! How then, do social work educators need to handle this issue? Are we justified, in allowing students to choose this area of social work practice (as an elective/specialization) and then not providing them the required support and recognition?

Where does the problem lie? Is it with the social workers

in workplace who have been silent performers, failing to fight for recognition? Is it with the industrialists and their important officials who find the entire idea of social work vague and irrelevant? Is it with the social work curriculum that probably does not do enough skill building, keeping the workplace as an area of practice in mind? Or is it with the social work educators who refuse to acknowledge and nurture this area of social work practice?

In industry, the clientele is different. Going by Maslow's need hierarchy theory these individuals mostly have their basic needs gratified but have other needs to be attended to.

Berry (1990) spells out:

> The practice of social work is usually looked at in its most narrow sense; a body of knowledge applying to the field of poverty. While this is importantly so, the other areas of application should not be ignored. Social work skills can be applied to various settings. The uniqueness of social work is that it combines values, skills and knowledge into practice. The comprehensiveness of social work education prepares a person to be a practitioner, not a philosopher. (p. 70).

It has to be realized that an industrial complex in its environmental and organizational climate is different from a social service agency. It employs a large labour force with a business objective. It has trade union organizations with internal or external leadership.

2.4.1. Identity and the Identity Crisis

There is an identity crisis for social workers in workplace – where do they actually belong, whether they need to be management oriented or social work oriented. This is also because for most of the industrialists social work is limited to tree plantation and medical camps. Very few of them know the profession, its objectives and utilities. Important functionaries, especially the line managers are mostly unaware of social work and its approach to human behaviour at work. They are confused with social work interventions–beginning from a proactive attempt of counselling a defaulting employee; since they feel fear psychology works and works easier. The professional social workers have to educate these key pins about social work interventions and its relevance in industry. In the light of these facts there is a need for joint effort of the academic institutions to promote social work principles, practices and techniques in industry.

There is the constant pressure of the potential (or actual) conflict between an individual worker's needs, the professional responsibility to these needs, and the organization's goal of expansion and profit maximization. Furthermore, practitioners are subject to the insecurities of organizational change. The experience of professional isolation in these unfamiliar and often intensely competitive circumstances heightens the difficulty. In more traditional settings (hospitals, public agencies, mental health clinics) social workers are surrounded by other trained professionals in the helping field who share common values. Such support groups are often not available to the industrial practitioner.

The social work practitioner in the work milieu is both an explorer and an entrepreneur. The workplace represents a complex system into which social workers have tentatively advanced, unsure of what needs exist and what welcome awaits. People in this setting although not hostile, are sometimes cautious, curious and unsure of what the social worker is there for or how best to use him or her.

2.5 Changing Paradigm of Social Work Intervention

As observed by Vigilante (1993):

> Assessment, common to all professional practice, is a dynamic process that continually takes in and

> discards information in an effort to order the multiplicity of ideas that are necessary to approach an accurate description of a client's situation (Lewis, 1982). Although many theoretical perspectives that social workers use are associated with a variety of treatment models, there continues to be a lack of clarity about the assessment process. Roberts (1917) identified "person in the environment" as the central social work focus. This psychosocial phenomenon permeates a variety of practice models and practice perspectives: the person-in-situation, ecological, life model, functional, crisis, problem-solving, task-centred, social functioning, structural, unitary, family, and social learning models among others (Bartlett, 1970; Epstein, 1988; Germain & Gitterman, 1980; Goldstein, 1981; Middleman & Goldberg, 1974; Perlman, 1957, 1970; Walters, Carter, Papp, & Silverstein, 1988). The other major principle in practice in models is objectivity. Both principles have been and continue to be central to the assessment process. However, whereas the essence of *psychosocial* phenomenon has persisted with minor changes in interpretation, the principle of objectivity has been subject to serious challenges by recent writers. (Anderson & Goolishian, 1988; Bateson, 1972, 1979; Bruner, 1986, 1987; Hoffman, 1990; Kelly, 1983). Changes in the value of this principle are evident throughout the various phases of intervention. As in all social work settings, the processes rest on the application of basic principles, values and techniques of practice modified by the setting. The other work setting offers some interesting challenges for practice that demand adaptations of established practice models. (p. 183).

The workplace of today is in the midst of vast changes. The combination is two-forth: advanced technology that is making work much simpler with the complexities of work life ever increasing. This is because the problems of living have become multifaceted. Globalization has brought with it lots of changes in various aspects of life. Some of the notable changes are: (i) Employment, workplace and workforce are undergoing tremendous transformation. Ever increasing number of women in the workforce has led to the unavoidable role shifts in the personal front, (ii) Open market economy has brought service sectors in light like IT, hospitality, BPO, which essentially require more educated workforce. In information Technology sector, many of the employees are professionally qualified. Being profit oriented as well as competitive, economic compensation and career progression is higher in these sectors but at the same time job security is low, (iii) Since Government has almost said farewell to welfare, its role as an employment provider has reduced drastically. The jobless growth of fast growing economy mostly due to the structural adjustment factor has put us in dark, (iv) Trade unions have either become subservient to other stakeholders or are virtually absent. Currently, their roles are limited. They are not able to defend increasing deployment of employee separation schemes in all sectors. In the present context trade unionism has to redefine its role and the nature of social dialogue has to be changed, (v) Due to the (consumer oriented) mass consumption approach, there is decrease in the savings propelled by changes in life styles towards increasing commercialism and attitude towards spending, (vi) a sizeable segment of the workforce is in sudden access to more money, flexi working hours, freedom, staying away from home and more proximity to the opposite sex at a young age; combined with consistent stress and competition at the workplace.

These changes are clubbed with organizational changes as explained by Leicht & Fennell (2001):

(i) Flatter organizational hierarchies as new information

technologies eliminate the need for middle layers of management.

(ii) The growing use of temporary workers employed on an as-needed basis to perform specific jobs for the duration of single projects.

(iii) The extensive use of sub-contracting and outsourcing to external firms and or suppliers to produce products and services that were once provided by permanent, in-house employees.

(iv) Massive downsizing of permanent workforce as organizations need less management and support people and replace unskilled workers with either computer-skilled operators or semi-skilled machine tenders.

(v) A post-unionized bargaining environment where unions have either no place or reduced power, and have no structural ability to gain a foothold to bargain with employers, and

(vi) Virtual organizations that exist as a web of technologically driven interactions rather than as a distinctive, physical work-site that can be concretely located in a geographical space. (p. 23).

A combination of these factors calls for a change in social work profession's approach to social work practice in the workplace. The neo changes have also brought more intense intra-personal and inter-personal problems at forefront. Increasing stress, financial mismanagement leading to heavy loans, problems in relationships at family and organizational level, dislocation, frequent job change and contractual nature of employment are a matter of serious concern. The impact is felt culturally, socially, economically and psychologically across all sections of workforce. The social work profession has to respond to these changes to keep workplace a vibrant social organization.

Mishra has aptly remarked:

> The need for change is further crystallized because there is increasing diversity of the workforce, the shift from manufacturing to an expanded service sector, rise in small workplaces which have been traditionally difficult to organize and replacement of regular male workers by part-time workers, shift in workers' skill levels and increasing proportion of highly educated and skilled workers who have little or no affinity to trade union movement, the general belief among such workmen that they can best deal with the problems of the workplace on an individual rather than a collective basis. (p. 25).

The social worker in workplace thus has to address concerns on diversity, ergonomics, disability management, and gender roles with both the spouses working, increasing marital conflicts, divorce rates, special groups and obviously more complex issues. There are also aspects such as HIV/AIDS, sexuality, EOE (Equal Opportunity Employment) that the profession has to address. It could be elaborated that social workers in workplace are necessitated to think for all the employees of the organization, and comprehend problems related to latest technological advances affecting the workplace. He may require the support of new methods and research to enable him to carry out his work diligently.

2.6. Conclusion

Social work in workplace has been under debate considering various factors such as nature of industry, the changing paradigms of the profession in the setting etc. However, the need for social work stems from these very factors.

As mentioned in the following words by Barak & Bargal (2000):

The challenge facing the profession is four-fold:

- Improve the fit between the needs of individuals and their families, work organizations, and communities.
- Help people in need of employment transition into jobs and become gainfully employed.
- Introduce to the workplace social work values and principles, such as valuing diversity and balancing family needs with work demands.
- Generate knowledge in the area of social work and world of work that will inform practice and policy. (p. 4)

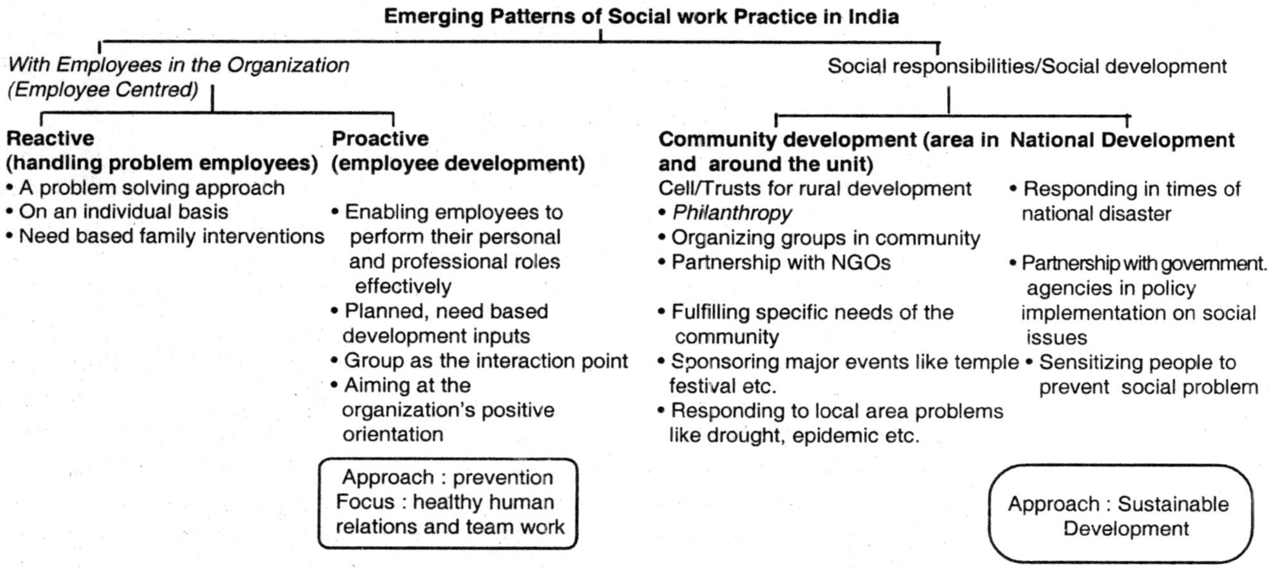

Fig. 2.1 : Emerging patterns of Social work practice in the Indian workplace.

3

Review of Literature

Any area which addresses the work, workplace and workers' well-being falls under the purview of social work in the workplace– especially labour welfare, personnel management, industrial relations, human resource development, training and development, working with unions, industrial counselling, occupational social work, employee assistance programmes, corporate social responsibility, working with specific groups, etc.

The focus of review has been, broadly, to highlight the literature addressing the area intersecting social work and the workplace. The literature reviewed has been classified and presented under two major headings: Studies in India and Studies in the West.

3.1 Studies in India

Since the time social work practice in workplace began with philanthropic concern towards workers' well-being, labour welfare has been its primary focus. Prior to independence, there were many individual and collective efforts to explore labour problems. The Royal Commission on labour may be considered as the first elaborate document bringing out issues and problems of the working class. In 1953, *The Indian Journal of Social Work* brought out a special issue on proceedings of

First All India Labour and Welfare Officers, which was held on April 3-6, 1953. **Acharya (1953)** emphasized that a philosophy of 'fundamental welfare' is needed to make labour welfare work meaningful. Such a philosophy aims at 'a system of society or a social reorientation that makes real and actively felt democratic living and full employment possible.' **Ahluwalia (1953)** argued that a *sound philosophy of labour welfare must be spiritual rather than materialistic*. **Edwards (1953)** defined the nature and philosophy of labour welfare as a branch of social philosophy. The original aim of creating wealth through industry was to promote human happiness and welfare. The means of creation of wealth has become an end in itself.

Gokhale (1953) explained industrial welfare programmes as a programmes that is not required by statute. It can be classified into six categories: education, housing, health and hygiene, financial aid and superannuation schemes, utilization of leisure, and improvement in factory working conditions.

Moorthy (1953) discussed that there is need for training labour and welfare officers because their job has grown in complexity and responsibility. This is consideration of the fact that they deal with human beings, function in consonance with business objectives, the progressing mechanical inventions; developments in social sciences and the labour organizing themselves into unions.

Moorthy (1953) elaborated that the philosophies and practices of welfare cannot be adequately discussed without going into the question of status of officers, since the status of personnel always influences their effectiveness or otherwise their functions. There is no uniformity in designations of personnel in industry. Thus, we have labour officers, welfare officers, industrial relations officers, personnel officers, employee relations officers and so on. **Vaid (1959)** defines the meaning of social work in industry, and makes a distinction between the social worker and the personnel manager. The tasks of the social worker in industry are divided into two categories: external and internal. Emphasis is laid on the necessity for right social scientists in industry without which they will hardly be able to do their work effectively. **Kochar (1960)** discusses the factory as a social system of management-worker levels of interaction and communication in a contract situation, with emphasis on interpersonal relations.

In the first detailed empirical investigation on *'Social workers in Indian industry'*, **Berkowitz (1962)** surveyed Labour Welfare Officers (LWOs) in and around Ahmedabad, to examine the role and function of the LWO. The responsibilities of LWO can be divided into four categories: (i) social work or welfare functions; (ii) maintaining and promoting harmonious relations within the plant; (iii) personnel or industrial relations functions; (iv) police function. Most of the LWOs, who believed that they are effective and attach importance to their roles as social workers, are recent graduates of social work institutions. LWOs are given too many jobs to perform and are not performing them. A consequence of the existence of the welfare officers in industry was that, it may be preventing the natural growth and development of the personnel functions in industry.

Hatia (1969) makes an urgent call for scientific personnel management in India. The role and responsibilities of personnel officers are explained and seen to be connected with (i) the objectives and tasks clearly entrusted to the personnel department, (ii) the resources made available for this purpose, (iii) the weight given to the advice of the personnel officer by his top management, and (iv) the authority given to him by top management.

Prof Jacob (1970) in his comparative study of the opinion of the personnel officers on the course content found lack of enthusiasm for the social work contents – both theoretical and practical – by those who had been taught social work subjects. The least wanted among the courses has been the generic training in social work without specialization in any field. Majority has stated that social work methods are very useful in dealing with the problems of absenteeism, indebtedness and indiscipline. The majority has also felt that there is scope for the appointment of full time social workers to start counselling and other social work programmes in the industrial settings. It was pointed out by many respondents that whether they were working as personnel officers or as welfare officers, the nature and load of their duties were such as to leave neither the time nor the disposition to carry out purely social work functions.

Verma (1970) discusses the labour welfare work of TISCO (now Tata Steel Limited) and its subsidiary companies. Some of his findings are: the city (Jamshedpur) had the proud privilege of obtaining services of the famous labour party leader **Sydney Webb**. As early as 1916 a committee was formed under his presidentship to prepare a plan for employees. The drive against drinking habit was taken up in 1962 by means of persuasion and other psychological approaches. The field staff in every unit was given special instructions in this regard. The organization came out with a separate department named as **Employee Service Section** (ESS) to provide advice and assistance to employees facing problems at and outside workplace. The ESS rendered useful services to the employees and their families. To combat the growing problem of indebtedness, a concerted drive against moneylenders was undertaken which yielded satisfactory results. The moneylenders were kept away from payment places, which also restricted their harassment of employees. The other major activities of ESS were mediation in family disputes, assistance in getting of ration cards, realization of credit society dues from ex-employees, service to employees who received summons and follow-up in compensation cases.

Menon (1974) found that awareness of social work training was quite satisfactory among the respondents;

absenteeism was rampant in most of the industries; alcoholism and indebtedness required professional intervention by the social workers. The study has not denied that some of the respondents have either negative or neutral attitude towards social worker. The study suggested that the academic institutions providing social work courses and the industrial organizations must co-ordinate between themselves and that the schools of social work need to orient and update industrial organization about social work practices in industry. The study also revealed the need to provide admission to the employees desirous to study courses offered by the schools of social work as sponsored candidates. The researcher foresees that such efforts would be useful in enhancing school-industry interaction and orient them in application of social work at the workplace.

Miranda (1974) pointed out that industrial social workers' status and their role as specialists has received much emphasis from the management and that the management exercises minimum control over their activities. The study also stated that application of social work methods are directly linked with their area of specialization. Social workers who had training in Family and Child Welfare or Medical and Psychiatric Social Work, dealt mainly with interpersonal problems and laid much emphasis on intensive social casework in comparison to group methods and community organization; whereas social workers trained in Personnel Management and Labour Welfare, paid much attention to group work and community organization methods in their working.

Srivastva (1974) found that there was a difference of opinion about the nature of relationship of the respondents with their labour welfare officer. An overwhelming majority (75%) of the respondents have expressed their relationship with the labour welfare officer as neutral, which throws light on his position of dilemma. Amongst remaining respondents, the number of respondents expressing their relationship with the labour welfare officer as strained is larger that of those who opined it as cordial. Similarly, only 6.5 per cent opined the behaviour of labour welfare officer as *fair* whereas 18 per cent regarded their behaviour as *unfair*. The majority (75.5%) remained undecided on this issue.

The period 1975-80 may be considered a turning point in the researches in industries as the period witnessed crucial changes. The imposition of national emergency in 1975, suspension of fundamental rights, introduction of workers' participation in management, emergence of HRD approach in management, formation and demise of the first non-Congress Government in the Country, irresponsible trade unionism etc., were some of the important events and characteristics of this period. Work and workers were studied in various perspectives. **Mahulkar (1976)** described: majority felt that counselling was very effective; many felt that the social workers were often more effective in the areas of family planning and welfare than in other areas. Majority preferred recruiting women social workers – especially married and in the age range of 26-30; they preferred professional social workers and said that knowledge of local language was essential; respondents felt that a pleasing personality, knowledge, skill and positive attitude were essential for a social worker and industries suggested that schools of social work should introduce industrial social work oriented theory and field work training. At the same time, it has been noticed that gender stereotypes attached to preference towards specialization at the Master's level underwent a vast change. Dhumale (1982) found that majority perceived that the major problems of an industry were alcoholism, absenteeism, indebtedness, health, work adjustment etc. largely caused by multiple reasons having its roots in family, bad habits and sickness. Majority preferred young, trained social workers experienced in social welfare agency, knowledge etc. to deal with their problems. They also recognized that trained social workers are more effective in family planning education.

Murthy and Patro (1977) studied the emerging concept of social responsibilities in industry with reference to Belpahar Refractories Limited, a joint venture of the Tata Group and Didier-Werke of West Germany. The company created a community social welfare department, which not only worked for physical, social, and structural development of these villages, but also became instrumental in raising the living standards of the villagers. The local population has been influenced to develop a spirit of cooperation and self-help, and the capacity to resolve conflicts at the village level.

Study in ten industries in and around Mumbai from various sectors was conducted by **Sinha (1990)**. His major findings were: (i) The perception of managements, trade unions and workers towards social workers is fairly good irrespective of the types of industry, qualification, designation and experience, (ii) Social work approach is the most effective in dealing with the personal problems of the employees: alcoholism, absenteeism, indebtedness, etc., (iii) Social workers are the most effective in carrying out all the welfare programmes meant for employees, (iv) Counselling is the most effective tool in dealing with industrial problems, (v) Casework and group work techniques are very much applicable and important, (vi) Social workers receive a good amount of co-operation from the management and trade union as well, (vii) Management gives importance to social workers' suggestions, (viii) The attitude of workers towards social workers is positive and favorable, (ix) Fieldwork practice in casework, group work and community setting is very useful, (x) Two years training in social work with labour specialization is much more appreciable and useful than generic course, (xi) Social workers face some limitations in performing their tasks such as job insecurity, less decision-making authority etc., but the management always tries to help them out. In general, a larger number of employees interviewed were noted to be satisfied with the practices.

Sehgal (1990) in her study based on 70 industrial units employing 100 or more workers in the districts of Indore, Ujjain, Dewas and Dhar in the State of Madhya Pradesh. Most of the management respondents were of the view that the functionaries employed in their organizations had only partially fulfilled their expectations. It appears that the social work trained functionaries seem to be doing their job in a better way as the level of fulfilment of the managements' expectations was comparatively higher where only social work trained functionaries were employed. Most of the workers were of the opinion that the functionaries employed in their units had only partially fulfilled their expectations. The highest percentage of those workers whose expectations were fully fulfilled belonged to small size units whereas comparatively more workers from the large size units stated that the functionaries had not at all fulfilled their expectations. The study revealed that many of the social workers did not find a conflict in the values of the industry and social work.

Srinivasan (1991) researched the issues related to social work practice in industries in 20 manufacturing organizations in and around the city of Madras (now Chennai). The study found that majority perceived the functions of the personnel officer as synonymous with that of the social worker. On the concept of social work, respondents' perception was that academic attributes symptomise the definition of social work in general. Awareness about specializations in social work is low. The appointment of full time social worker finds favour among majority. The lack of social inclination on the part of the managements and the problems of role identification of social work in industry, are perceived to be the major reasons for the dearth of social workers in industrial organizations. Majority desired that social worker should be on the pay roll of the industry. Counselling and personal guidance were identified as the two preferred areas for intervention by social workers. Generally, the level of knowledge and awareness about professional social work is low. Across the categories of respondents, there seems to be little doubt as to the role and utility of the professional social worker in industry. **Desai (2002)** also studied perceptions of 120 professional social workers, who graduated from Faculty of Social Work, M.S. University, Baroda. It emphasized remodelling of social work education to meet the challenges of the rapidly changing Indian corporate world. The study found a direct relationship between the courses studied and role performance. Knowledge acquired by professional social workers from the background courses such as Human Development, Psycho Pathology, Introduction to Social Sciences, and Philosophy of Social Work were found to be utilized adequately in their jobs. It was also found that communication; human relations and counselling skills were perceived as the most relevant for providing direct services to the employees, be it in the field of human resources, personnel, administration, industrial relations or welfare services. Out of the three major training components – theory, research and field work at the masters' level, 109 respondents perceived that fieldwork helped them in acquiring the skills, whereas 74 of them perceived that theory helped them and 54 respondents perceived that research helped them in acquiring skills. Significant relationship was found between experience of respondents and their attitude towards training.

Saxena (2004) describes that if social functioning is adversely affected, and if the disturbance in social effectiveness is the primary problem, the responsibility is clearly that of the profession of social work. He reiterates how high socio-economic status does not necessarily mean that the 'individual is fit' and low socio-economic status does not necessarily mean that the 'individual is unfit'. For example, in an organization a manager with a sound socio-economic status might suffer from nervous breakdown, or stress due to family or job related problems. He emphasizes that any individual in the society can suffer from problems and that professional help of the social work professional is needed in every section of the society.

Shetty (1993) studied an industry's approach to alcoholism and alcohol related problems and found that there are also some covert and indirect causative factors of alcoholism that are observed. One is the corporate practice of serving alcohol at parties hosted for managers and even at training programmes for many employee cadres including foremen and also reimbursing liquor bills under entertainment expenses. At the annual departmental picnics, liquor is served. Subtle peer pressure to join the group and have alcohol cannot be denied at such events. It is evident that the intervention of the counsellors plays a crucial role in propelling the alcoholic to accept treatment with the use of specialized techniques like educating, providing warmth and support to the alcoholic and his family when needed. The other powerful strategies used are crisis precipitation and modifying home and work environment of the alcoholic. **Sundar (2000)** focused on Indian business philanthropy through the ages. The findings to the study are as follows: (i) there is a shift from merchant charity to corporate citizenship; (ii) many corporates are practicing social responsibility and contributing to social welfare; and (iii) the corporate should keep the institutions of civil society alive and promote individual freedom, social justice and civil responsibility by supporting non-profit groups engaged in such work.

Siddiqui and Sukhramani (2001) presented a detailed account of the development and recent practice of occupational social work in India. The article reviewed the industrialization of India and the subsequent legislations instituted in the country. There are some ideological differences about the practice of social work at workplace.

The dilemma before the industrial social workers is to whether they have to become pro-management or pro-worker. There are two models of service delivery in the workplace – institutional and community based. While the former entails work within the confines of the industrial organizations, the latter locates the social worker in the colonies inhabited by the industrial workforce.

The review of literature revealed that there are not many studies directly addressing social work practice in industry in India. The subject on social work practice in the workplace in India has been researched by select researchers at different time periods. Interestingly, most of these studies were done for higher research degree by social work educators in India and most of these studies have also been taken up by women. The review indicates the following trends: (i) Scanty research on relevance of social work education in industrial setting, (ii) lack of exclusive study on the practices of professional social workers in workplace from professional engagement perspective. In the Indian context there are not many empirical studies on various aspects of social work practice but the issue has been studied at different intervals.

3.2. Studies in the West

Unlike India, in Western Countries, social work practice in the workplace has been welcomed by different stakeholders. The literature reviewed has been divided into two broad categories: writings available on the subject *Social work in industry* in the first category and researches on various specific components related to practice of social work in industry in the second.

Explaining the rationale for industrial social work, **Heidberg (1954)** in *'Factory and Family'*, differentiated the word *'and'* between 'factory' and 'family': (i) both are a single unit or (ii) both are separate units, and (iii) there are mutual relations between factory and family. The author agrees with the third meaning because the worker is at the same time a member of his family as well as the factory. Both social patterns have their specific order and laws, but both are living through the same factor, the worker. Therefore, overlapping is unavoidable, and the problem is to find the right way by which the requirements of both institutions are met. In this direction lies: (i) the contribution the family has to make to the factory, and also (ii) the task of industrial social policy and social work. Industrial social work can be directed to: the working sphere, the living sphere of workers, and the relations of living sphere and working sphere. **Powell (1957)** in '*Recent trends in industrial sociology*' presented an account of how industrial sociology has developed three aspects of attention: (i) Human relations in the industrial plant, (ii) relations between industry and community; and (iii) relations between industry and society. It is normally argued that this field lacks adequate theoretical framework, which exists in face of some partial frameworks explaining particular settings.

Hanlan and Jocobs (1969) elaborated that social work has pointed out the conspicuous absence of private industry in the fight against poverty. Social work tends to be elitist in its 'ascription of knowledge and values, only to social workers.' It is pointed out that there are many problems that can be taken on by a coalition of social work and private industry.

Skidmore et al. (1974) presented a brief description and analysis of a promising innovation in social work – provision of social services in a large corporate industry. The social services, begun in 1969, are available for workers and their families. Four aspects of the development of social work in industry are illustrated: (i) professionally trained social workers provide services to a client group that heretofore was not reached, (ii) the employment and support of social workers by corporate leaders creates a promising opportunity for jobs and the provision of social work services, (iii) the cooperation of corporate leaders, social workers, and community agencies augurs well for increased community coordination in both the delivery and the effective utilization of services, and (iv) social work education needs to adapt to this new thrust in the provision of social work services in both class-work and field-work placements.

Akabas (1978) advocated that social work skills have become highly relevant to corporations and unions, as they have expanded their function into the social welfare arena. Selection of appropriate sites for field work placements requires an ability to make an assessment of organizational readiness. Careful selection of students and clarity of social work function at the field site contribute to successful outcome. In addition, back-up support from the school, including recruitment of interested faculty, field supervision, and new curricula, is essential to the smooth development of these innovative and stimulating placement opportunities.

Steiner and Borst (1980) advocated an expanded role for social workers in US industrial settings. Three basic motifs that characterize industrial settings are briefly delineated: (i) increasing financial and material rewards; (ii) increasing therapeutic services; and (iii) increasing systemic restorative and preventive services. Social workers in the US have not done enough to make industrial representatives aware of social work services useful to them and their employees, and too little attention has been paid to making social workers aware of opportunities for service in industrial settings. **Morton (1981)** stated that current discussions of social work roles in industry have centred on applications of interpersonal practice methods. While community development has not traditionally been associated with organizational practice, it is suggested that there is a basic similarity in values and approaches between Organizational Development (OD) and Community Development. **Popple (1981)** presented a review on '*Social work practice in business and industry*' during 1875-1930 and mentioned that the number of social workers hired by business and industry has increased in recent years. The social work profession has taken a great interest in this phenomenon, hailing it as a new and promising field of practice. Examination of social work in industry, from its beginning in the late 1800s to its demise in the late 1920s, demonstrates that, far from being a new field of practice, this was one of the earliest specializations.

Neikrug (1982) examines issues relating to the meaning of work for the worker and clinical implications for the social worker intervening in the field of industrial and occupational social work. The problems of work dissatisfaction and alienation in work are analyzed. Two concepts - *work* as play and *logo* therapy - are useful in clinical intervention in work-related problems. **Tudiver (1982)** mentioned the rise of application of business management techniques to social service programmes. It is argued that social workers need to ground their actions in a solid understanding of the political and economic context in which they work. To this end, the contradictory position of social workers in their roles as professionals, managers and workers is analyzed.

Abramovitz and Epstein (1983) emphasized that as capital is increasingly channelled to the private sector from the public sector in the USA; social work has become increasingly privatized, causing changes in welfare policy. It is argued that this has obscured the role of the social worker and caused a shift from social work's historic commitment to client well-being to concern for private enterprise. The growing tension within the discipline is outlined by examining: (i) the trends in privatization of social welfare policy and services; (ii) conflicts that arise when social work is practiced in corporate settings; and (iii) how the field at large responds to them. Should the tension between social work values and those of industry ever recede the profession's progressive political basis will be lost to the conservatism of the *status quo*.

Frank and Streeter (1985) presented a conceptual

framework that demonstrates the broad range of skills and activities appropriate for social workers in industrial settings. The framework indicates the levels at which social work intervention can occur within the industrial setting and the importance of both micro and macro level skills for industrial social workers. **Marlow (1991)** explained the extent of occupational social work in Great Britain and its inclusion in social work education. Based on responses from 20 institutions offering Master's degree social work programmes, the study indicates that occupational social work as a field and employee assistance programmes as well are not developed to any great extent in Great Britain. However, employment-related services are beginning to grow in response to a broad range of needs and problems. **Balgopal et al. (1997)** concluded that "... as Singapore develops from a colonized state to a thriving economy, needs of the labour force are also changing. Market forces, societal progress, and stress at the workplace all make industrial social work a necessity rather than a luxury." **Gustavsson and Balgopal (1991)** used mail questionnaire data received from 75 accredited US schools of social work to explore how they perceive their role in the preparation of social workers to assume professional responsibilities within work settings. They remarked that although social workers are increasingly entering work settings, including employee assistance programmes, there have been no dramatic increase in the number of specialized occupational social work programmes. Despite the small number of schools with such a specialized concentration, an overwhelming number do incorporate this content in their broader curriculum.

Resnick (1985) examined the application of social work skills in the industrial sector. An intervention designated as shadow consultation that uses traditional casework and group work skills to help individual managers become more effective and humane in their work, is described.

Trice (1986) reviewed the historical development of Employee Assistance Programmes (EAPs) to help alcoholic and other troubled employees. It is contrasted with other workplace movements to help employees (example industrial social work, employee counselling, occupational mental health). EAPs are contrasted with other current workplace interventions, quality of work life demonstrations, and health promotions. Particular emphasis is given to the conflicting occupational claims for expertise made by practitioners. Current research on the constructive confrontation strategy used in EAPs are reviewed and critiqued, and suggestions are offered for future research.

Reichert (2003) in *'Workplace mobbing: A new frontier for the social work profession'* described that in the US, abusive work environments perpetrated by a group against a target individual are well documented. Some European countries refer to this group action at the workplace as 'mobbing'. Mobbing can occur in any work environment and often leads to adverse emotional and other effects on both the individual and society as a whole. Because social workers are involved in workplace issues, they should be familiar with mobbing. However, the social work literature in the US does not address this issue. This article defines mobbing, examines characteristics and effects of mobbing, and explains why mobbing is a human rights violation.

Gettman and Pena (1986) discussed of occupational social work in the US-Mexico border region in terms of the gender, cross-cultural, and systemic factors that affect workers' mental health. The Border Industry Programme (BIP) is discussed and implications of the maquiladora programmes for the labour force are described. Three major challenges for social workers in this setting are identified: (i) raising sensitivity to the bilingual-bicultural character of the population, (ii) gaining access to industrial settings without losing autonomy, and (iii) networking with other health professionals on both sides of the border. An important concern is knowing when to challenge the very structure of the industrial organization to promote health in the workplace.

Cunningham (1990) described that as a field of practice, occupational social work has been greatly influenced by identification with employee assistance programmes and their typical focus on the chemically addicted employee. It is contended that this merger of two separate service models requires a clarification of roles and functions and a redefinition of the problem focus and treatment options in contemporary, work-based programmes. **Googins (1987)** discussed the development of what is now known as Occupational Social Work (OSW) in the US through five stages: (i) welfare capitalism, (ii) personal problem orientation, (iii) service model, (iv) prevention model, and (v) organizational change. Some major issues confronting the field at present are discussed, including: (a) determination of who is the client, (b) intervention into micro or macro problems, (c) boundary disputes, and (d) the role and control of treatment. Some future directions for OSW programmes are outlined in the light of the impact of political, professional and SE forces. **Maiden (1987)** added that social work practice in work settings, particularly employee assistance programmes, has experienced substantial growth over the past decade. With this growth arise a number of practice issues related to the professional conduct of social workers in work-based social programmes and the impact these programmes have on public social services. Other relevant issues are client self-determination and degree of confidentiality. **Danto and Mazzella (1988)** attempt to assist social workers in Employee Assistance Programmes (EAPs) who often find themselves isolated. Professional support and problem-solving groups have been established in recent years in the New York City metropolitan area. Here, the peer supervision model is presented, and illustrated *via five* case examples. Group formation, structure, and dynamics are discussed. It is anticipated that peer supervision will become the model of choice as EAP practice becomes generalist. The peer group model creates a greater sense of community among occupational social workers than any traditional supervisory hierarchy could. **Straussner and Phillips (1988)** brought out a historical analysis of the ambivalent and fluctuating relationship between social work and organized labour in the US, with focus on the period from the 1870s to the 1940s, when frequent shifts between cooperation and strife were most dramatic. It is shown that these fluctuations paralleled changes in social and political values. While the current relationship is a mutually beneficial one, the fragile nature of the link between organized labour and the social work community cannot be ignored, particularly in the light of the increasing involvement between social work and private industry.

Taylor et al. (1988) discussed key process questions in their work *'Paving the way for EAP evaluations: Implications for social work'*. It is assumed that: (1) non-threatening process-type questions may be used in helping EAP evaluators' plan their evaluations; and (2) the profession of social work can meaningfully assist in developing and answering such questions. **Stoesz (1989)** states that social welfare professionals have been reluctant to take advantage of administrative opportunities in the rapidly growing corporate human service sector. For profit human service firms offer advantages that welfare professionals should consider as methods to advance social welfare, example, employment opportunities, and access to capital, programmes innovation, and organizational change. At the same time, proprietary human service delivery presents troubling issues: preferential selection, unfair competition, and industry consolidation. Social administrators electing to work in the proprietary sector must find ways to reconcile opportunities with these issues.

Van (1999) said that many families are subjected to the

routine separation of a family member, example business executives, sales representatives, military employees, and politicians. Described here is a new occupational social work intervention that assists families in resisting the stress of separations, that is, that increases their "separation resilience".

Mudrick (1991) sees that the role of occupational social worker is underdeveloped as far as the employment of *people with disabilities* is concerned. He mentioned that, although occupational social workers routinely assist employees with alcohol or drug related problems, workers with disabling problems such as back pain, paralysis, and cancer have not received much attention.

Lewis and Lewis (1989) found that community counselling model provides helping professionals with guidelines to design comprehensive intervention strategies for assisting businesses and their employees with the transition process. The components of the model include: (i) direct client services such as individual and group counselling; (ii) indirect client services such as client advocacy, consultation, and training; (iii) direct community/ organization services such as stress management training, career development and life planning workshops, transition awareness training, newsletters, and retraining; and (iv) indirect community/organizational services focusing on the interface between the environment of the workplace and the employees working in that environment.

Puder (1980) discussed the increasing number of employee counselling programmes and the critical issues underlying their credibility. The critical issues for credibility include: (1) a programmes appropriate to the structure and needs of the organization; (2) a code of ethics; (3) outreach efforts such as employee education and supervisory orientation activities; (4) staff qualities and skills; and (5) a "mental wellness" approach, which focuses on the maintenance of adaptive functioning and prevention of serious problems.

Mor-Barak and Tyman (1993) referred that it is a new challenge for occupational social workers to work with older workers and the workplace. They found that the trend toward early retirement, coupled with the diminishing numbers of youths entering the labour market as a result of lower birth rates, presents US industry with an impending shortage of available workers. Concurrently, many older adults can anticipate a prolonged and healthy aging and are interested in continuing their productive involvement in society. However, older adults face many difficulties in obtaining and retaining a job, the most important of which is age discrimination. Here, several areas for social work intervention are suggested to promote continued employment and rehiring of older workers, including advocacy, linking older job seekers with interested employers, advising companies on work arrangements and training programmes, and counselling older workers and their families.

Workplace problems and needs for lesbian and gay male employees were studied by **Van (1999)**. The research was based on a conceptual model for framing workplace interventions addressing issues of protection, inclusion, and equity for gay/lesbian employees. Research findings indicated that heterosexual employees greatly underestimate the level of discrimination that sexual minorities experience; women respondents were more sensitive to gay/lesbian workplace issues than men; existing EAP (Employee Assistance Programmes) and human resource services, programmes, and policies inadequately address gay/lesbian needs; significant differences exist between heterosexual and gay/lesbian employees on perceptions of diversity training content and gay/lesbian

Du Plessis (1994) explored that occupational social

workers are stuck in tertiary level casework; efforts to humanize the workplace and to challenge organizational factors that hinder an ecological practice metaphor.

Csiernik (1996) discussed the historical failures and potential benefits of social work interventions at the workplace. Since the advent of the industrial revolution, most workplace programmes have not pursued worker well-being as a primary goal, but as a means of enhancing efficiency. In recent decades, workplace assistance programmes have emphasized the identification and coercion of problem employees, rather than examining and transforming the environmental factors that contribute to worker dissatisfaction, ill health, and emotional distress. Despite some progressive changes, most social work has adhered to these trends and failed to establish a proactive presence in the workplace. It is suggested here that social workers must seek worker and community wellness in addition to increased organizational productivity, addressing individual worker needs and problems while serving as an intermediary between labour and management.

Zapusek (1998) stated: starting with an outline of Straussner's models of social work, it is found that help to the employers or the company itself is the most developed model at the Velenje Mines, Slovenia. The five components of the project, Control of Disability, are presented: (1) disability control awareness and legislative framework promulgation, (2) disability prevention policies development, (3) employee-focused programmes, (4) professional rehabilitation, and (5) the implementation of a disability control system in the workplace.

Leighninger (2000) reviewed two articles from the archives of Social Work Today written in the 1938. The first is by Martha Winters, "Now I am a CIO Organizer" (1938). Winters was a social worker in a small town for 15 years before becoming a CIO organizer. The leaders of the small community had brought some industry into the area and encouraged the workers to beware of labour unions. The workers, however, were in favour of the unions but found that the smallness of the community made it harder to make change. The CIO educated the community as it went along. Social workers were able to help facilitate change.

Moxley (2002) discussed that social workers who offer employment services can frame job development and placement as a process of workplace socialization in which they facilitate the inclusion of people with disabilities in mainstream work settings. This paper examines the construct of workplace socialization and offers five specific strategies and related tactics for its facilitation in the context of social work practice in disability and rehabilitation.

Corporate social responsibility is another area, which has witnessed steady growth. This area also requires the interventions of social work professionals because of its components. **Hamilton et al. (1980)** described that the concept of social responsibility as applied to business suggests that the corporation no longer has a responsibility only to the stockholder but must make decisions aimed toward balancing the interests of all clientele groups affected by actions of the corporation. These groups include managers, administrators, employees, and the general public. The relationships among employee characteristics, industrial setting, functional position, perceptions of actual responses to social demands, and employee expectations of responses were investigated by surveying individuals in boundary spanning positions in four industrial settings. Findings suggested that organizations had failed to meet employees' expectations concerning their social responsibilities.

3.3. Conclusion

The feasibility of social work practice in the workplace has been debated across the globe for many years now. While earlier labour welfare was considered social work in the workplace, the trend has changed with newer concepts emerging in human resource development. The literature above indicates the need to study the nature, extent and types of social work practices in select industrial organization of Indian conglomerates with a tradition for social work and the professional social workers working in these organizations.

4

Tata Organizations and Social Work

Profile, Perspectives and Practices

Tata Group – An Account of Welfare and Development

4.1. Introduction

With over 200,000 employees across 93 operating companies, the Tata Group is one of India's largest employers in the private sector. Founded by Jamsetji Tata in the 1860s, the Tata Group's early years were inspired by the spirit of nationalism. The business operations of the Tata Group currently encompass seven business sectors – Engineering, Materials, Energy, Chemicals, Consumer Products, Services and Communications and Information Systems. The scale of the Tata Group's operations is increasingly turning global.

4.2. Tata Group – Historical Development

Jamsetji Nusserwanji Tata, the founder, came to Bombay at the age of 14. In 1868, he launched the famous Empress Mill in Nagpur. Later, he launched the Swadeshi Mills to mark the beginning of the Swadeshi movement (a movement to popularize the use of indigenous goods as opposed to British goods, which marked an important forward surge in India's struggle for freedom). The Tatas pioneered India's first steel industry; started the first power plant in India; pioneered civil aviation in India; brought insurance to India – the New India Assurance Company in 1919; started India's first chain of luxury hotels; led commercial vehicle production; led India's software development efforts; launched India's first passenger car and introduced labour welfare benefits long before they were enacted by law.

4.3. The Tata Family: The Pioneers

A brief account of people who with their visionary leadership spearheaded the Tata Group is discussed in the ensuing paragraphs:

(a) *J.N.Tata :* In 1892, Jamsetji endowed a fund for deserving students for their higher education abroad. He envisioned a national system of education, a premier institute for research and education in the fields of science and technology, medicine, philosophy and the arts. In 1898, Jamsetji offered to set aside 14 of his buildings and four landed properties in Bombay for an endowment to establish a university of science. In 1905 the government agreed to meet half the cost. The Indian Institute of Science opened in 1911 in Bangalore, many years after Jamsetji's death.

(b) The Taj chain was set up because Jamsetji wanted luxury hotels that did not discriminate among its guests, unlike some British establishments that had signs saying "Indians and dogs not allowed". Jamsetji's Taj venture is distinct from his other schemes. He had no desire to run the enterprise – unlike his other enterprises. He built it to attract people to India. The Gateway of India was yet to be built when the Taj rose in its solitary grandeur facing the mouth of the harbour. In his foreign travels, Jamsetji made most of the Hotel's purchases himself – a soda and ice making factory, washing and polishing machines, a laundry, lifts and an electric generator. The first building in Bombay to be lit by electricity, the Taj opened in 1903, in Jamsetji's lifetime. During World War I (1914 to 1918), the hotel was converted into a 600-bed hospital.

(c) *Sir Dorabji Tata* : Sir Dorabji saw through the establishment of the Indian Institute of Science, Bangalore, which was to spearhead scientific research in India for decades to come. He was knighted in 1910. As President of the Indian Olympic Council, he financed the Indian contingent to the Paris Olympiad in 1924. He supported the Non-Cooperation Movement in South Africa in 1912, led by a then relatively unknown lawyer – Mohandas Karamchand Gandhi. He extended financial support to Gopal Krishna Gokhale, to set up the Servants of India Society.

(d) *Sir Ratan Tata* : Sir Ratan endowed a house at Shantiniketan for European research scholars coming to India to study the oriental literature and culture. He funded the first archaeological excavation at Pataliputra between 1913 and 1917, which resulted in the discovery of the 100-column Mauryan throne room in Ashoka's palace. In 1912, he encouraged the University of London to institute a Chair at the London School of Economics to investigate and research into the causes of destitution and poverty.

(e) *JRD Tata* : The concept of establishing Asia's first cancer hospital in Bombay was implemented under his guidance in 1941. JRD's contribution to the scientific establishment came in 1945 when he gave the founding grant to Homi Bhabha to set up the Tata Institute of Fundamental Research. JRD Tata was drawn to the cause of population control. He part-funded Avabai Wadia's efforts in initiating the Family Planning Association of India. In 1970, he started the Family Planning Foundation jointly with the Ford Foundation. For his endeavours in the field, JRD Tata was bestowed with the United Nations Population Award in 1992. JRD's passion for flying was fulfilled with the formation of the Tata Aviation Service in 1932. The first flight of Indian civil aviation took off at Drigh Road airfield in Karachi on October 15, 1932. JRD Tata was awarded the country's highest civilian honour, the Bharat Ratna, in 1992 – one of the rare instances when the award was granted during a person's lifetime. And, on his death, the Indian Parliament was adjourned in his memory. His home state of Maharashtra too declared three days of mourning when he passed away on November 29, 1993.

(f) *Naval Tata:* Naval Tata was nominated to represent the Indian textile industry at a meeting of the Geneva-based International Labour Organization (ILO). He became a part of the ILO's governing body in 1951 and continued in the post till his demise in 1989. He was a member of the International Organization of Employers, also based in Geneva, for 38 years and was the President of the Employers' Federation of India from 1959 to 1985. Naval Tata was the driving force behind the setting up of the National Institute of Labour Management (now known as the National Institute of Personnel Management), serving as its President from 1951 to 1980.

(g) *Ratan N Tata :* Ratan N. Tata joined the Tata Group in 1962. He was named Chairman of Tata Industries Limited in 1981. In 1991, Ratan N. Tata was appointed

Chairman of Tata Sons Limited, the apex body of the Tata Group.

4.4 The Tata Values

The main aim of the Tata Group is to improve the quality of life of the communities it serves. The founder of the Group believed that "our heritage of returning to society what we earn evokes trust among consumers, employees, shareholders and the community. This heritage will be continuously enriched by formalizing the high standards of behaviour expected from employees and companies".

The five core values of Tata Group are :

- *Integrity*
- *Understanding*
- *Excellence*
- *Unity*
- *Responsibility*

4.5 Social Initiatives in the Tata Group

What prompted the founders of Tata Group to invest in social initiatives? The Tata Group has travelled a long journey: from corporate philanthropy, to welfare, to corporate social responsibility and now to corporate citizenship. Its journey has been abstracted from its historical development by the researcher, as follows:

(i) *Envisaging a Long-Term Impact on National Welfare*: 'Don't just give, but give to build'. Jamsetji did not want to practice what he termed the 'patchwork philanthropy' that just gave handouts to the poor. That had its place, he acknowledged, but the expertise and resources of businessmen like him were better employed developing leaders and larger projects that would have a lasting impact. This was realized through (i) Tata Trusts and (ii) Institutions such as TISS, IISc etc.

(ii) *Bequeathing Most of One's Personal Wealth to Philanthropic Trusts:* In 1898, foreseeing the importance science would play in the new century, he pledged half his personal wealth for the creation of a top-of-the-line educational institution for science. In 1911 this was realized with the Indian Institute of Science, IISc, the precursor to the IITs that has helped change the image of India today.

(iii) *To Ensure Sustainability of Such Initiatives:* Through all the family's bequests, the Tata Trusts now control 65.8 per cent of the shares in Tata Sons, the holding company for the group. Therefore, with every Tata enterprise, it is well known that a large percentage of profits are bound for philanthropy – the companies pay dividends to these trusts as shareholders, which are then ploughed back into philanthropy. Tata Sons holds the bulk of the equity owned by the Group in the share capital of its key companies. The chairman of Tata Sons is traditionally regarded as the Group chairman. The company is the owner of the Tata name and the Tata trademarks that are registered in India and several other countries and are used by all Tata companies in relation to their products and services.

(iv) *Individual Organizations to Contribute to Realizing the Group's Purpose: To improve the quality of life of the communities it serves:* The philanthropic philosophy embodied in the Trusts has to be followed by all the group companies. This is realized through creating a nodal organization called the 'Tata Council for Community Initiatives' (TCCI), to coordinate all Tata Companies in meeting their social responsibilities and the Tata Human Development Index to benchmark the contributions of Tata companies towards social development and environment protection. The cost for social initiatives comes from the companies themselves.

The Tata Group has adopted a two- pronged strategy – channelizing funds thereby making their social initiatives sustainable and simultaneously making huge investments in the field of education and research. While the Group has created systems to achieve its mission, it has also evolved numerous institutions for feedback, monitoring, evaluation and corrective measures. The forthcoming paragraphs give a brief account of some of their approaches, organizations and institutions:

4.5.1 *The Tata Trusts*

There are two principal trusts operating under the Tata umbrella: (i) Sir Dorabji Tata and allied Trusts and (ii) Sir Ratan Tata Trust.

(i) *Sir Dorabji Tata Trust:* Sir Dorabji always believed that wealth must be put to constructive use.A few months before his death in 1932, Sir Dorab bequeathed most of his personal wealth comprising substantial shareholding in Tata Sons, Indian Hotels and allied companies, his landed property and wife's jewellery, including the famous Jubilee diamond, twice the size of the *Kohinoor* and estimated at Rs.1 crore (10 million) even his pearl-studded tie pins and cuff links to the newly registered Sir Dorabji Tata Trust – for the advancement of learning and research, the relief of distress and other charitable purposes. This was the beginning of the Sir Dorabji Tata Trust.

Over 75 per cent of the Sir Dorabji Tata Trust's funds come from dividends on the shares it holds in Tata Sons, the Group's holding Company. The remaining comes from their statutory investments. The Trust does not handle CSR but is more of a funding agency. It supports different kinds of NGOs – social work, research, community based usually for a period of three to five years. It also works with international agencies such as the UN at the time of natural disasters. It also initiates from time to time, the process of establishing institutes of national importance. The Trusts do not usually encourage or consider supporting projects run by Tata Companies. The Trustees' view is that, if a company has started something, then it should sustain itself through its own funds instead of asking the Trusts for financial support. The trust is best known for promoting six pioneering institutions of national importance. Four of these were established in Mumbai: the Tata Institute of Social Sciences (1936); the Tata Memorial Centre for Cancer Research and Treatment (1941); the Tata Institute of Fundamental Research (1945) and the National Centre for the Performing Arts (1966). The National Institute of Advanced Studies (1988) and the Sir Dorabji Tata Centre for Research in Tropical Diseases (1999) are in Bangalore. Other than these, the trust continues to promote projects in livelihood, the management of natural resources, health and other areas of social development.

(ii) *Sir Ratan Tata Trust:* Sir Ratan died in 1918 and he left directives in his will for his personal wealth to be used for basic and advanced education, primary and preventive health, rural livelihood and communities, art and culture and public initiatives, for all Indians, at a time when almost all trusts were communal in nature. Sir Ratan Tata Trust was set up the same year.

> Sir Ratan Tata Trust depends on dividends from its Tata Sons shares and its investments. It supports NGOs, individuals and institutions, and the areas it touches are rural livelihoods, health, education, arts and culture, and civil society and governance. Though the focus has shifted from charity to development funding, the provisions of Sir Ratan's will are still the Trust's principle guidelines. It utilizes its funds in five areas: basic and advanced (post-graduate) education; primary and preventive health; rural livelihoods and communities; arts and culture; and public initiatives. Preference is given to projects based in rural India, and those that involve the advancement of women and children.

Between themselves, the Tata trusts have created an infrastructure for the balanced development of the nation in science, technology and the social sciences. They have given India its first institute for social sciences, its first cancer hospital and research centre, and its first institute for fundamental research, which gave India a head start in its atomic energy programme. 'Allied Trusts' comprises of (i) Tata Social Welfare Trust, (ii) R D Tata Trust, (iii) Tata Education Trust, (iv) JRD Tata Trust, (v) JRD Tata and Thelma Tata Trust, (vi) Jamsetji Tata Trust, (vii) JN Tata Endowment, (viii) Lady Meherbai Tata Memorial Trust and (ix) Lady Meherbai Tata Education Trust.

4.5.2 Tata Council for Community Initiatives (TCCI) – A Collective Effort for Corporate Social Responsibility

Tata companies have largely contributed to the development of the communities around their areas of operation. TCCI was established as a result of the need felt within the Tata

Group to co-ordinate all Tata Companies in meeting their social responsibilities. It was recognized that these objectives could be better realized by the sharing of experiences, collective learning and enhanced participation. The TCCI mission is as follows: *We will evolve a common direction for community development programmes from diverse activities of all Tata business units through sharing and participatory networking. We will strive together constantly to strengthen our professional and organizational abilities to fulfil our commitments towards society at large.* TCCI has been created on the following objectives: (i) To promote concept of corporate citizenship in all Tata Companies. (ii) To reinforce voluntary efforts in community development and (iii) To increase awareness of programmes that enable communities to become self-reliant. The council is the apex body in the Tata group to provide direction and management support for corporate social responsibility and environmental management of Tata companies. It is structured to be a network of representatives from the Group Executive Office, senior Tata Directors and Executives along with working level facilitators. The Council facilitates the process of establishing the tenets, core values and processes for carrying out community development activities.

The TCCI facilitates Tata Companies to meet their social responsibilities through usage of their resources, skills and talents; co-ordinates activities of Tata Companies through regional groups to initiate and sustain community development; formulates specific policies, guidelines and organizational arrangements for building strong sustainable communities and evolves a common direction for the Tata Group's environmental initiatives. TCCI acts as a nodal agency to review traditional social work, raise funds, and mobilize volunteers and synergies strengths within the Tata Group by pooling technical and managerial resources and employee time. It formulates specific policies and organizational arrangements for building strong, self-reliant and sustainable communities.

It annually reviews the community programmes and the overall social performance in the Group as an integral part of the Tata Business Excellence Model and under the Tata Brand. TCCI operates through a secretariat from Tata Services to ensure that this effort is forwarded as a Service. The TCCI focuses on: water management; vocational training; literacy programmes; family health schemes; waste management and computer education. Many of these issues are tackled by networking and co-operating actively with government agencies and NGOs.

TCCI has evolved the Tata Guidelines for Community Development and now coordinates the process of implementing them through autonomous regional groups. TCCI regional groups plan to mobilize more volunteers, institute systems and methods for selecting and running programmes for greater impact on the community and initiate a convention by which to measure their performance. At a Group level, TCCI has been reconstituted to include Tata Directors, CEOs and senior executives in order to help integrate the Tata way on social responsibility as part of the Tata Business Excellence Model and in the spirit of the Tata code of conduct. TCCI has also formed the Tata Group Environment Network to evolve a common direction for the Group's environmental initiatives.

Employees are in the core of activities of TCCI as the live wire of values. Corps of volunteers is the institution through which TCCI facilitates the process of taking talent to the under privileged. The community facilitator or champion has a key role to play as a source of leadership. He or she creates more leaders within the company. TCCI governance mechanism is decentralized, open, transparent and at the same time simple. It includes: (i) a council comprising of fifteen members including Group Executive Office (GEO) members,

(ii) an executive committee consisting of six guardian CEOs and six regional coordinators, (iii) action in regional groups which again has six chief executive officers and six regional coordinators and 191 champions, (iv) projects run by Tata employees through the team comprising the chief executive officer, HR heads, champions and volunteers and (v) volunteering by Tata employees – the main focus, the source of initiative and talent: the institution.

4.5.3 Tata Index for Sustainable Human Development

Tata Group has developed tools and techniques for its better implementation and monitoring. The Tata Group has evolved a CSR index, which is known as the *Tata Index for Sustainable Human Development*. The index has been prepared by TCCI to benchmark the contributions of Tata companies towards social development and protection of the environment.

The TCCI worked closely with United Nations Development Programme to develop this index, which establishes a correlation between the Tata Business Excellence Model and the UN's human development index. Group companies are required to undertake a points-based self-evaluation based on several criteria such as leadership commitment, strategy development, review mechanism, employee involvement, volunteer schemes, and managing change. They have to rate their performance on these parameters on a scale of 0-1000, called the 'scale of human excellence', which has five sub-bands, namely, human consideration (scale: 0-250), human concern (251-450), human achievement (451-650), human development (651-875) and human excellence (876-1000).

If a firm is at the 'human consideration' stage (scale: 0-250), it means its CSR activities are rudimentary. A firm in the 'human concern' band is "still evolving its value system" while at the next stage (human-achievement), its employees demonstrate a high degree of realization, accomplishment and capability for collective action. The human development stage is a state of realization that building a community is central to human survival and growth while the 'human excellence' goal is the self-expression of people who have a quality of life that is a benchmark for others to emulate.

4.6 Profile of Tata Organizations Studied: At a Glance

4.6.1 Titan Industries Limited, Hosur, Tamil Nadu

Titan Industries was incorporated in 1984 as joint venture between the Tata Group and TIDCO (Tamil Nadu Industrial Development Corporation) Limited, a Government of Tamil Nadu undertaking. The Company has its registered office in Hosur, and industrial town in Tamil Nadu and its Corporate Office in Bangalore, Karnataka. In 1994, Titan Industries diversified into jewellery. Manufacturing operations are carried out at Hosur (Tamil Nadu) and at Dehradun (Uttranchal). The major products of the Company include quartz wristwatches, jewellery and quartz timepieces. Titan jewellery is sold under the brand name 'Tanishq'. It has a trade union named the *Titan Employees Union* and it is not politically affiliated. The union is involved in shaping and executing community welfare.

4.6.2 Tata Infotech Limited, Mumbai, Maharashtra

Tata Infotech Ltd. is part of the multi-billion dollar Tata Group, with 74 per cent of company shares being held by the Tata Group, and the remaining 26 per cent by the public. Tata Infotech was called Tata Unisys till 1997. In September

1997, Unisys divested their shareholding to the Tata Group, as a result of which the company name was changed to Tata Infotech. Tata Infotech has since then built-up its own customer base but continues to work closely with Unisys. Tata Infotech has built a considerable base of its own. The organization is a global systems integrator and also manufactures hardware and provides education services. It has no trade union.

4.6.3 Tata Motors Limited, Pimpri, Pune, Maharashtra

Tata Motors (formerly TELCO – Tata Engineering and Locomotive Company Ltd.) was established with the primary objective of manufacturing rail locomotives at Jamshedpur in Jharkhand (then a part of Bihar), in 1945. Vehicles began rolling out from Tata Motors, Pune in the year 1977. The third plant was set up in Lucknow in 1992. At present, Tata Motors functions from Jamshedpur, Pune, Lucknow, Mumbai and Dharwad. It is India's premier and only fully integrated automobile manufacturer. It is also among the world's top 10 producers of commercial vehicles. Tata Motors enjoys a significant demand in export markets such as Europe, Australia, South East Asia, the Middle East and Africa and its vehicles currently sell in over 70 countries. Tata Motors is India's only vehicle manufacturer with product offering in all three segments – commercial vehicles, utility vehicles and passenger cars. The trade union is *TELCO Employees' Union,* and it is not politically affiliated.

4.6.4 Tata Refractories Limited, Belpahar, Orissa

It is located in Belpahar, Sambalpur District of Orissa state. Belpahar in Orissa stands 537 kilometers from Calcutta on the main Howrah-Mumbai railway line. Belpahar was almost unknown in the industrial geography of Orissa till 1957. In 1958 B R L, one of India's biggest and most modern refractory plants, was set up in joint collaboration of the Tata Iron and Steel Company [(TISCO), now called Tata Steel], and the Didier Werker A.G., West Germany, the largest manufacturer of quality refractories in Europe. One of the important factors for choosing Belpahar as the site was to develop the under-developed areas of Orissa. The product range includes refractory and refractory products. *Tata Refractories Shramik Congress* (TSC) is the only trade union and it is also not politically affiliated.

4.6.5 Tata Steel Limited, Jamshedpur, Jharkhand

Created in the year 1907, Tata Steel was formerly known TISCO. It has been an example of pioneering initiatives in labour welfare, personnel management, industrial relations etc. Tata Steel is India's largest integrated private sector steel company. Its steel plant at Jamshedpur produces four million ton of hot and cold rolled flat and long products. Tata Steel is one of the few Indian companies to be invited to join the UN-sponsored Global Compact. It has also been conferred the prestigious Global Business Coalition Award (GBC) for Business Excellence in the Community in view of its outstanding work in the field of HIV/AIDS awareness. Jamshedpur was India's first planned industrial township. In more recent times, Tata Steel has received ISO 14000 certification for environment management for most of its works, plants, mines and collieries.

4.6.6 Tata Tea Limited, SIPO, Munnar, Kerala

Tata Tea Limited plantations in South India are located in the Western Ghats – in the eastern part of central Kerala and an adjoining part of Tamil Nadu. The former, mainly in

Devicolam Taluk of Kerala's Iddukki District, is known as the High Range. The other estates in Coimbatore District, Tamil Nadu and one estate in Trichur District, Kerala, form part of the Anamallais plantation area. In 1964, a collaborative venture between the James Finlay Group, the pioneers in tea cultivation, and the Tatas, the pioneers in Indian Industry, was initiated to develop value added teas and in 1976 Tata Finlay Limited purchased the black tea producing/ marketing operations and other interests. The name of the company was changed to Tata Tea Limited in 1983 when the James Finlay Group sold their remaining shareholdings, including the considerable hectarage and manufacturing facilities in northeastern India. Today, Tata Tea Limited is the largest integrated tea company in the world, with activities spanning the entire spectrum of the industry.

The product range includes agriculture the plucking operation; manufacture – green leaf is converted into black tea in the estate factories; marketing – the CTC production is being packed and marketed internally throughout the country. Packet Tea – Tata Tea Limited is the first producer in South India to start its own polypack operations. There are five recognized trade unions in the organization (2 for staff category and 3 for workers and supervisors). This is the only organization among those studied which has five trade unions, also politically affiliated. The union representing Staff and Special Category employees of the Company (i) Estates Staff Union of South India and, (ii) National Union of Plantation Staff are affiliated to INTUC and AITUC respectively whereas union representing supervisors and workers of the company known as (i) South India Plantation Workers Union – an affiliate of INTUC (ii) Devicolam Estate Workers' Union is affiliated to AITUC and (iii) Devicolam Peermade Estates Supervisors Association is affiliated to INTUC. All the above Unions, except NUPS, were recognized in the late 1950s. The exact dates of recognition are not available. NUPS was recognized in 1979.

The researcher found that the Tata Group has pioneered employee development and social development in many ways thereby contributing to national development. The Group's social initiatives indicate the importance of visionary leadership that firmly believes in the social role of business. It also appears that setting personal examples by way of bequeathing wealth and initiating large-scale projects is crucial for business participation in development. It appears that the group encourages employee volunteers for social initiatives at a large level; interventions were need based in relation to the business of the organization; absence of publicity to social initiatives; consistency of efforts and that social initiatives were coordinated under the Tata Council for Community Initiatives (TCCI). Therefore it can be said that the Tata Group has been pioneering and attempting in its own way social initiatives with the belief that its business has to bring about positive change in the lives of its employees, community and the country.

Social Work Practice in Select Industrial Organizations

On the basis of discussions above, one can find a correlation between the approach of Tata group towards nation building and the philosophy of social work. The core values of the Tata Group are concerned with employee and societal development. Towards employee development, the Tata Group has gone beyond the statutory welfare measures adopting progressive and proactive human resource management practices. With national development as its vision, the Tata Group has focused on developing the community in and around its workplaces. A close analysis of the strategies of the Tata Group indicates that employee development and social development are largely being integrated into the long-term goals of the organizations. The Group has attempted corporate social responsibility in various types of welfare and development programmes intended for special groups like women, disabled, senior citizens etc. A diagrammatic representation of the Group's social work philosophy and strategic roles are given in figure 4.1.

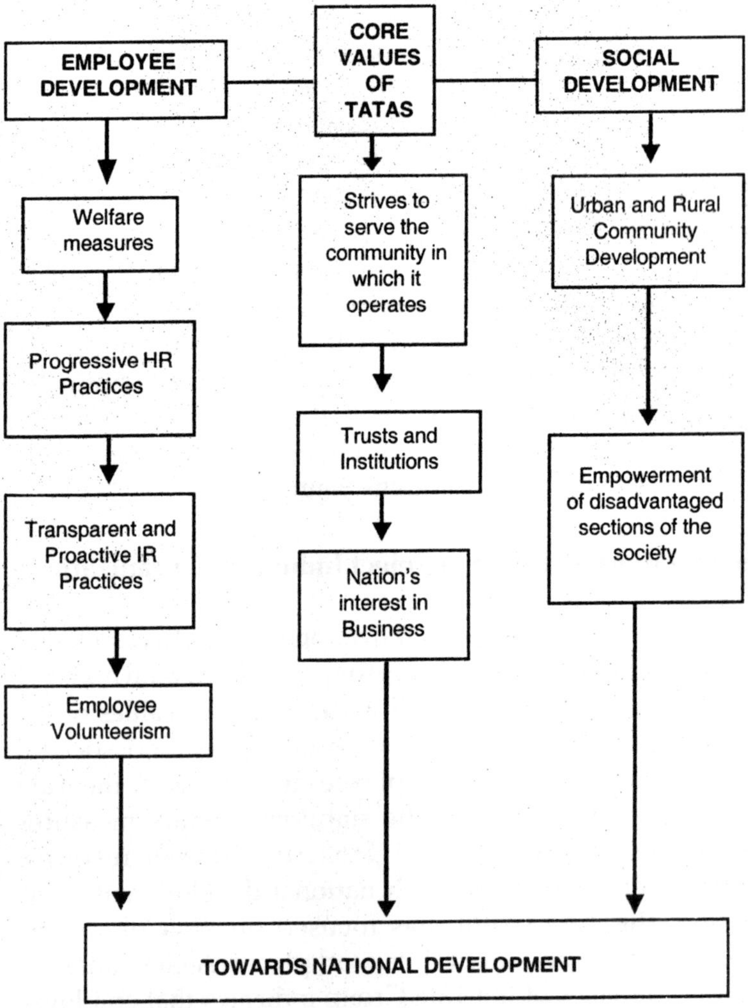

R. Nalini: 2006

Figure 4.1: Social Work Philosophy of Tata: An Overview

Social work practices in industrial organizations studied are broadly brought under four classifications: (i) employee welfare – statutory and non-statutory, (ii) family welfare, (iii) welfare of special groups and (iv) community welfare. Accordingly, practices in the select organizations are described below:

4.7.1 *Statutory Employee Welfare*

The Tata Group has been a pioneer in implementing welfare programmes in their organizations. Long before the government assumed the role of welfare state and entered into legislative protection, many provisions of different legislations were already in practice in Tata Group of industries. The researcher observed that five out of the six organizations studied provide housing, schools and hospital facilities to their employees. The other welfare amenities provided by all organizations were conveyance, recreation, holiday homes, sports, etc. The researcher wishes to highlight many welfare firsts of Tata Steel Limited, (formerly TISCO) given in Table 4.1 that were subsequently enacted as laws by the Government :

Thus, the Tata Group has the unique distinction of introducing welfare measures that were at that point of time non-statutory, but later on became guiding lines for government action.

4.7.2 *Non-Statutory Employee welfare*

While statutory welfare ensures good working conditions and conditions of work, Tata organizations have initiated various programmes within and outside the workplace mostly not covered under any statutory provisions. Some of the significant programmes are:

(i) *Employee Counselling*: Counselling was practiced in

Table 4.1 From Tata Group to the Nation: Some Welfare Firsts

S. No.	*Particulars*	*Introduced at TISCO in (Year)*	*Enforced by Law in (Year)*	*Legal Enactment*
1.	8 hour working day	1912	1948	Factories Act
2.	Free medical aid	1915	1948	Employees' State Insurance Act
3.	Establishment of welfare department	1917	1948	Factories Act
4.	Schooling facilities for children	1917	None	None
5.	Formation of Worker's Committee for handling complaints concerning service conditions	1919	1947	Industrial Disputes Act
6.	Leave with pay	1920	1948	Factories Act
7.	Workers' Provident Fund Scheme	1920	1952	Employees Provident Fund Act
8.	Workmen's Accident Compensation Scheme	1921	1961	Workmen's Compensation Act
9.	Technical Institute Apprentices, Craftsmen and Engineering Graduates	1921	1961	Apprentices Act
10.	Maternity Benefit	1928	1946 /1961	Bihar Maternity Benefit Act 1946 & in 1961 by Govt. of India
11.	Profit Sharing Bonus	1934	1965	Payment of Bonus Act
12.	Retiring Gratuity	1937	1972	Payment of Gratuity Act
13.	Ex-gratia payments for road accidents while coming to or returning from duty	1979		
14.	Social audit	1980	–	First in India
15.	Pension scheme	1989	–	

all the organizations in various forms. One organization had counselling cell in the HR Department – the focus areas being post-retirement counselling, career counselling, higher studies etc. A grievance-handling cell for redressal of officers' grievances was also present. The Head of HR department was in charge of this cell. In another organization, HR officers counselled workers in distress with a view to helping them help themselves. For this purpose, help was also taken from the concerned departmental head whenever necessary. Counselling was provided to employees for absenteeism, productivity improvement, substance addiction, indebtedness, marital discords, attitudinal change etc. It was a continuous process in which the HR officer was involved. One organization had services of a professional social worker for providing counselling for the benefit of employees – to help them gain capabilities that would impact not only in their work but also throughout their life. Ethics counsellors were also present to address all new entrants on the Tata Business Code of Ethics. This Code of Ethics talks about dos and don'ts for individuals in their role as employees of Tata.

(ii) *Loans/Small Savings*: Loans are granted to deserving employees for building houses, purchase of two-wheelers and four-wheelers, refrigerator, furniture etc., and for meeting expenses on sickness and for education of children. Almost all employees have enrolled themselves under Pay-Roll Savings Scheme.

(iii) *Privilege Leave in Anticipation*: In case an employee has no privilege leave (but has accrued privilege leave), he would under specific circumstances like ill health of self, examination, marriage of self etc., be sanctioned PL in anticipation. This is subject to a maximum of 15 days and on two occasions in a year.

(iv) *Upgrading Knowledge*: Tata organizations encourage its employees to acquire additional technical or professional qualifications. This is done by providing partial reimbursement of expenditure incurred towards tuition fees, examination fees and cash awards. Certain courses are listed for this purpose. Employees desirous of acquiring additional technical/professional qualifications are provided assistance.

(v) *Library Facilities*: It was observed that organizations have a central library that caters mainly to technical and managerial reading, and also has some fictional works.

(vi) *Financial Security:* The Employees Mutual Benefit Fund and the Parivar Suraksha Yojna provide financial assistance to the employee in case of permanent disablement and the employee's spouse or dependent member of the family in case of death of the employee.

(vii) *Healthy Life Programme*: This scheme is applicable to all confirmed employees, 35 years and above, irrespective of their grades. Employees in the age group of 35 to 44 years undergo the check up every alternate year and employees aged 45 years and above undergo the check up every year. This scheme is also applicable to an employee's spouse, whereby he/she can undergo the check up every year, if he/she is 45 years of age and above. This is irrespective of whether the employee is eligible for this check-up or not. The costs of these check-ups are borne by the organization. It also reimburses the conveyance expenses from residence to hospital and hospital to office/residence (as the case may be), to the employee/spouse. The medical report of the employee/spouse will be handed over to the employee for further action and follow-up.

(viii) *Supporting Higher Education*: Objective of this policy is to facilitate employees achieve higher proficiencies, Diploma, Degree, Post-Graduate Degree/Diploma and/or Doctorate which would also help enhance skill pool and meet the future business requirements of the company. This scheme is applicable to all confirmed employees of the company.

(ix) *Programmes of Social Importance:*

(a) *Encouraging Adoption:* Employees who adopt a child will be eligible for maternity leave up to a maximum period of twelve (12) weeks to get adjusted with the baby, subject to application for leave being given well in advance along with proof of adoption.

(b) *Promoting Kitchen Garden*: Workers are provided with land, wherever available, free of cost, to maintain a kitchen garden of their own.

(c) *Better Living Services*: Besides free homes, some of the organizations provided their employees with free electricity up to prescribed limits.

(d) *Promoting Animal Husbandry*: In Tata Tea Limited, the company encourages cattle rearing, with a view to ensure that a supply of wholesome milk is available to the workers and their families. The company at a very nominal fee provides cattle keepers to look after the cattle and cattle sheds necessary grazing land. A veterinary department is also maintained to render medical aid to cattle owned by employees. The services of qualified artificial inseminators are also available to the cattle owners.

(x) *Incentives and Encouragement*: In Tata Tea Limited, employees are provided hot tea by the management, free of cost, every day at their work spot. Staff and special category employees are issued with free dry tea as a monthly allowance. In Tata Steel, lady executives are provided 15 additional days privilege leave, preferential house allotment for working couples, metro allowance for metro employees, free water and medical facilities, subsidized electricity, housing to all employees and monetary incentives for employees acquiring higher education in related field are provided. Besides these, there are many other benefits: group health insurance scheme (Domiciliary and Hospitalization); extra leave for maternity; death relief scheme; welfare fund; free watch (one at the time of joining); loans and advances; gold coin – long service award; township and school and two increments for additional qualifications; long service award; suggestion awards; man of the month and man of the year awards; good attendance award; home visits by officers in the event of joy or sorrow in the family of employees by HR officers and immediate supervisors; family education; yoga classes in factory premises; lectures on physical fitness to employees above 40 years of age and legal aid to employee.

(xi) *Rehabilitation Committees:* With a view to helping the employees injured while on duty or otherwise and employees suffering from chronic or serious illness a Rehabilitation Committee comprising 15 officers and 2 Union Representatives has been set up. The committee deals with the following types of cases: (i) Helping an employee who is injured on duty by giving him light duty during the healing period as per the advice of the medical department, (ii) Helping an employee who has developed permanent disability to perform his job by providing alternate and suitable work.

(xii) *Canteen and Credit Societies:* One organization had its canteens run by the co-operatives of employees. There were four such co-operatives. All the employees including the officers eat the same food. These societies are paid for their services, the infrastructure and raw materials being provided by the company. The canteen employees have also formed their own co-operative societies for rendering various services. Other co-operatives include credit and industrial co-operatives. With a view to promoting managerial skills amongst its employees, and to create employment opportunities for their dependents, industrial co-operatives were set up at the initiative of company's workers with the encouragement of the management. The societies are run entirely on the principle of self-help. The land, the labour, the investment all belong to the shareholders of the Society and the Company provides only the technical know-how. The company also gives them raw material wherever necessary and acts as a ready market for them.

4.7.3 Family Welfare

Family has been one of the focus of the attention of Tata philosophy of welfare. Family planning had been the area of intervention till 1970 and later on the focus progressed to family welfare. All confirmed married employees of the Company and their spouse are covered under this scheme. The employees who undergo a permanent family planning operation are paid an incentive of Rs.1,000/- This is also extended to the employees' spouse who undergoes the family planning operation. In addition the employee will also be entitled to a special leave for six working days immediately after the operation. The other interventions which are either family focused or for family are :

(i) *Employee Family Visits:* Out of six Tata organizations, employees' family visits are practiced in four organizations. Employees could bring their family members for a factory visit on the day earmarked for it every week. Family members are brought in by company buses from various localities. They are welcomed by the concerned Divisional Heads at a small function and a film on welfare activities is screened for them. Officers of the company as well as union leaders address them and answer their queries. The volunteers of the division take them around the factory premises in groups. Lunch is served in the canteen and then they are dropped back by the buses in the city.

(ii) *Assistance for Children:* Expenses towards purchase of textbooks for school going children of employees who successfully pass in the final examination of the previous academic year are reimbursed.

(iii) *Parents' Meet:* This forum was introduced to establish rapport with the newly recruited employees. Divisional Heads along with all the supervisory staff attend the meet. The office bearers and representatives of the union also participate along with their families. The Divisional Head while welcoming the parents familiarizes them to the company's culture and its working style. The meet ends with a factory visit by the parents on the following day.

(iv) *Child Merit Scholarship:* The objective of this scheme is to promote the education of children of employees through the grant of scholarships by the company. The scheme applies to all employees from the date of joining the company. Two children of each employee, aged 2 to 21 years, who are admitted to a Nursery/School/College, shall be eligible for grant of a scholarship under this scheme.If the employee is in India and his/her child/children are studying overseas, he/she would be entitled to CMS (in Indian rupees).

(v) *Scouting Facilities:* Children of plantation workers are provided facilities for extra curricular activities such as scouts, bulbuls etc.

(vi) *Link Workers:* Link workers are volunteers selected from the workers to assist in the health and welfare programme of the estates, and to provide a link between the management and the workers. The purpose was establishing two-way communication channel between the health department and management and the workers and to bring about participation of workers in the estate health and welfare programmes. The subjects covered in the training programme are approach to the family; recording of data regarding personnel residing in each house; assisting in the maintenance of records and registers; maternal and child health and family planning; nutrition; environmental sanitation; personal hygiene; commonly prevalent diseases; home economics; communication skills; occupational health; first aid; productivity and absenteeism; leadership and training programme; fuel conservation and organization of cultural and sports activities.

(vii) *Family Register/Card:* A comprehensive Family Card (earlier Family Register) is maintained for every worker. Complete information of the family is collected which includes number of family members, age, gender, educational status, employment status, relationship with the worker, health status, blood group, permanent address, marital status of children, family planning details and miscellaneous. The card is updated every year to record additions and deletions to the family. The other registers maintained are eligible couple register and 'Under 5 register'. These cards and register serve as a vital source of information.

4.7.4 *Welfare of Special Groups*

It is believed that real welfare lies in taking care of the needs of special groups that are vulnerable. In all spheres of life, there are special groups seeking assistance and are in need of special care and protection. The Tata Group has catered to the welfare of special groups in its programmes keeping in mind their work and well-being. Some of the Group's programmes are:

(i) *Employment Opportunities to the Disabled:* Titan employs 117 disabled persons in the blue-collar workforce in Hosur. For selection of the disabled, Titan Industries undertook identification of tasks, classification of tasks, and appropriate recruitment processes. Once the tasks capable of being performed by the disabled had been identified, they were categorized into those that could be performed by individuals where the nature of disability would still enable them to perform the desired task. Appropriate selection procedure for each type of disability was adopted. Considering aspirations that might not be satisfied at a later stage of the individual's career, disability-related limitations in career opportunities were conveyed to the individuals well as their families. The disabled were housed with others, in an attempt to integrate them with the rest of the workforce. Fortnightly meetings were held with the disabled to address issues of their specific concern. The supervisors were trained in the use of sign language. To address the special needs of these employees the following steps have been taken: training to enhance their technical competence, computer literacy; non-discrimination in all policies and creating a conducive work environment by ergonomic working area, effective grievance handling, counselling etc.

(ii) *Srishti Complex:* With the objective of training and rehabilitating the children of employees found to be mentally or physically challenged, Tata Tea has various projects. The complex earlier housed a mushroom factory of the company. When it was closed due to various reasons, utility of the infrastructure available was discussed. The idea of using it for a developmental cause was suggested and accepted. A survey was conducted into the needs of the workers. A team consisting of labour welfare officers, doctors, field officers under the auspices of the Industrial Relations Department carried out the exercise. It emerged from the survey that a large number of employees' children were either physically or mentally challenged (the reason could be attributed to congenital marriages). The fact that both the spouses are employed in the company meant that these children were left at home with no one to attend to them. A large majority of them had never attended schools or undergone any sort of training. Keeping these factors in mind, 'Srishti' was carved out. The following projects are functional at the Complex:

(iii) *Developmental Activities in Rehabilitative Education (DARE Project):* Children with physical or mental impairment having learning disabilities are imparted special education and related services. Awareness programmes and counselling for parents are conducted at regular intervals. The school has seven special educators who are employed by the company. The staff has been trained at National Institute of Mentally Handicapped and 'Reach' an NGO working for the differently abled in Calcutta. Each child admitted into the school is put through a selection procedure. The mentally challenged children have an IQ (intelligence quotient) assessment done. Accordingly, they are grouped and training given. All the children are given free uniform, tea, healthy lunch and snacks.

(iv) *Strawberry Unit*: In order to rehabilitate the mentally challenged children trained at DARE, a strawberry preserve-making unit was started, where a number of these youngsters are engaged. Marketing of the strawberry is arranged by the company.

(v.) *Aranya and Athulya: Aranya* unit provides vocational rehabilitation for youth with physical disability. Under *Athulya,* there are two units are operating: (a) Vocational Training Centre for Physically challenged children which provide training and rehabilitation. The unit produces envelopes, books, pads, files etc. Tata organizations ensure procurement of the product from this unit. The unit has successfully completed 15 years of operation. In similar way, the hand-made paper unit was started functioning 1999 to make hand-made paper and other paper products such as cards, envelopes, writing pads, paper bags, photo frames, penholders, tablemats etc. Company vehicles are provided to transport them from their place of residence to the complex and back. The profit made from these centres is given to the employees who are designated as trainees. It is important to mention that *Srishti* is not an NGO, but a welfare wing of the company, and that its profits are ploughed back to the centres.

(vi) *Domestic Management Programme :* Domestic management programme initiated by Tata Steel's HR and Corporate Communications departments aims at covering every Tata Steel family and large community around its operations. The programme is conducted as workshops and seminars to household ladies focusing on: interpersonal relationship, positive thinking, domestic safety, health and environment improvement, women's rights and duties, drug and AIDS awareness, domestic budgets, parenthood.

4.7.5 *Community Welfare*

The Tata Group has given importance to community welfare in its industrial organizations. In five organizations studied, the researcher found separate departments for social initiatives in varied forms and under different titles such as department of community development and social welfare, department of social initiatives, department of community development etc. Some organizations had classified their activities under community development and rural development. The underlying philosophy behind such initiatives was to in move the quality of life of communities in which they operate. Generally these departments cover various villages in and around the unit focusing on integrated rural development. The Tata Group has adopted various approaches towards community welfare and community development. It has its own department and it has also entered into partnership model. Some of the successful models of the organization are cited:

(i) *Community Based Business Opportunity:* Under this programme, Tata organization has entered into partnerships with non-governmental organizations. MYRADA, an NGO that was facilitating the women's self-help groups requested Titan Industries for a contract to its women self-help groups – the job of laundering uniforms of its employees. Titan had a job (bracelet assembling) to sub-contract and required legal entity to which it could make payments for doing the job. MYRADA organized the women to become owners-managers-workers of their own enterprise. The women were organized into informal task groups with 8-10 girls in each group. Each group had a bank account in its name and Titan paid into these accounts directly. Later in 1998, as per the legal and financial experts' advice, all the women came together and registered as a company called MEADOW. Task groups rather than individuals hold the shares of the Company. A representative holds the shares in her name and the other members of the group are listed as co-owners. Titan has extended its support in the following areas: manpower selection (among the target community identified by MEADOW), on the job training of manpower at in-house facility, sharing SAP system through the dial-up mode, for data entry and documentation, training in material accounting and documentation procedure and lending work tables, tools on free of cost and returnable basis.

(ii) *TANSI (Tamil Nadu Small Scale Industries Corporation Limited):* TANSI is a state government undertaking established to promote the small-scale sector. The watch assembly Unit was primarily established to provide job opportunities for women living in a tribal area. TANSI has been looking for sub-contract of similar nature to retain employment of their women workforce. Titan supported TANSI by offering sub-contract of watch assembly operations. Titan has extended its support in the following areas: technical training, SAP connectivity for data entry, material accounting and documentation, investment in equipment and has placed one representative to assist TANSI in following systems and procedures as per Titan's requirement.

(iii) *TELCO Grahini Udyog:* TELCO Grahini at Pune started in 1973 as an organization for the women, the aims of which were to provide work for women. The

TELCO Grahini movement was started so that housewives were provided with an opportunity to work in the spare time available to them. All grahinis are shareholders of their respective co-operative societies, so in effect they are their own employers. The housewives participate in all the organizational and production activities of the Grahini Udyog. Whenever deemed necessary the company imparts special training to enable those concerned to be able to discharge their duties efficiently and this is a continuous process.

(iv) *Tata Relief Committee:* In November 1974 the Jamshedpur based Tata Relief Committee (East) was incorporated. Spearheaded by Tata Steel, the TRC (East) also includes Tata Steel's sister concerns, associate companies and Jamshedpur industries. The objective of TRC is to render help to those affected by natural calamities by offering them food, medical aid, rehabilitation etc.

(v) Life-line Express : TSRDS has been involved with the Life-line Express also called 'Jeevan Rekha'. This is a fully staffed hospital on wheels equipped with modern operation theatre to provide diagnostic, medical and surgical treatment for prevention and curative interventions for the handicapped. Tata Steel got involved with the Life-line Express in India in 26.08.1991. Since then TSRDS has hosted it on two more occasions in Jharkhand.

4.8 Tata Policies on Social Issues

In addition to human resources policies such as recruitment, selection, promotion etc, Tata organizations have framed written policies on social issues of significance such as drug de-addiction, HIV / AIDS etc.

(i) Policy on HIV POSITIVE Status and AIDS Control : The HIV / AIDS employment policy in brief adopted at Tata Motors is :

No HIV test at pre-employment stage: It is felt that at the entry point, it may not be feasible to test each individual, as apart from the fact that the test currently available is fool proof; the prior permission of the candidate is required for administering it.

Detection and treatment of HIV positive status during the course of employment: As soon as the company receives information regarding an AIDS case, the following action will be taken:

(a) *Secrecy:* The company will maintain complete secrecy about the case as HIV positive status carries a serious stigma.

(b) *Employment:* The employee will continue to work based on the medical opinion that the affected employee can perform his normal work.

(c) *Follow-up:* The employee with HIV positive status shall report to the Medical and Industrial Health Officer of the company at least once in three months for medical check-up.

(d) *Medical expenses:* It will be reimbursed by the company according to the limits laid down in the medical scheme.

(e) *HIV positive employees who are unable to work:* When the HIV patient is unable to perform his normal duties he will be advised to seek voluntary retirement on medical grounds.

(ii) *Alcohol and Drugs Policy:* Tata Steel believes that the loyalty and commitment of its employees depend upon the quality of life they are offered at work and at home. Recognizing that indiscriminate use of alcohol and drugs is injurious to the well-being of individuals, their families and community as a whole, Tata acknowledges that the misuse of these psychoactive substances is a major health and safety hazard. Tata Steel is committed to creating an alcohol and drug free environment at the workplace. This would be achieved through the involvement of all employees and the Joint Department Councils in spearheading appropriate initiatives. The initiatives would include (i) raising awareness, through the dissemination of information, education and training and by promoting healthy life styles among our employees and their families and (ii) Motivating those employees who have an alcohol/drug problem, to seek assistance, while maintaining confidentiality about such cases.

(iii) *Policy on Equal Opportunity Employment:* Tata has policy of non-discrimination with respect to gender and non-employment of child labour. In keeping with the Tata code of conduct conscious attempts are made to provide equal employment opportunities to all potential applicants without discrimination on basis of gender. No child labour is employed under the Code of Conduct and there is no verified incidence of non-compliance with child labour laws.

(iv) *Policy on Employee Volunteering Scheme:* All organizations promote volunteering scheme for its employees with the following objectives: inculcating an attitude of giving back to the society; contributing to the deployment of community development policy to address the needs of local communities and strengthening internal loyalty and sense of fulfilment of the employee.

(v) *Policy on Social/Welfare Audit:* The management of Tata Steel thought it important to have an evaluation of its social activities conducted. Tata Steel appointed a

> three-member committee consisting of Justice S.P.Kotwal (chairman), Prof. Rajni Kothari (a social scientist) and Professor P.G. Mavalankar (a public man with Parliamentary experience) to examine and report the extent to which the Company has fulfilled the purpose laid down in Clause 3A of the articles. The Committee submitted its report in 1980, which was published by TISCO under a separate cover and not as a part of the annual report for the year.

The system of Social Welfare Audit in Tata Tea Estates in South India began in 1986. Since then it has been an annual feature for the comparative assessment of health and welfare inputs on individual estates and their impact on the dependant population. The evaluation is based on two-fold inputs – Health and Welfare; data collected from each Estate by its health and welfare team and a physical verification is carried out by a welfare audit team comprising of an eminent External Auditor, the Deputy General Manager (IR), the Chief Medical Officer, and the Medical Officer in charge of Community Development and Social Welfare Scheme. At the end of the audit, a meeting of all senior executives, estate managers, medical officers and welfare officers is held with the external auditor and two way dialogues take place discussing various possibilities for improving the quality of life of the population. A consensus is reached on the future welfare measures to be undertaken. An evaluation sheet and a score sheet are sent to the estates in advance, so that the estate is aware of the assessment criteria. Instead of visiting particular areas as suggested by the Estate, the welfare team visits areas chosen by means of lot at the time of arrival on the Estate; this can avoid special preparation for the purpose of the audit.

Welfare Committee comprises of all labour welfare officers, select doctors and one representative from all relevant departments. The Committee meets once a month to discuss welfare and health issues. The Committee later sends the minutes of the meeting to the General Manager who takes appropriate action. Estate Level Welfare Committee includes the welfare officer, field officers, medical officer, manager and assistant manager of an estate form the Committee. The Committee meets whenever need arises. The quality and frequency of the meetings is assessed through perusal of the minutes and it forms an important assessment criterion in the annual welfare audit.

4.9 *HR Practices Needing Special Mention*

Recruitment from rural institutions is another policy adopted by some of the Tata organizations. The Titan Industries, recruited non-management level employees immediately after their SSLC/HSC/ITI directly from institutions in *villages in Tamil Nadu* through psychological, aptitude and other tests. The aim was selection of outstanding students that resulted in an average of one out of every one hundred and four students.

Tata follows the *Buddy System for induction,*which helps the new employee to settle down smoothly at the new place. The 'Buddy' is a friend, who takes the new comer around, shows them what's what and who's who, and facilitates and smoothens the process of induction. The existing employees who may have faced problems at the time of their joining and would like to share their experience to help new comers to settle down with ease at the new place to come forward and become a Buddy.

As far as issues related to transparency and openness in communication are concerned, there are various schemes and practices in an attempt to encourage openness and transparency in communication. One organization had its managing director visiting homes of employees across grades – mostly the workers. He speaks to the families of employees and spends approximately half an hour at each home. The HR head or the Head of Training Centre accompanies the MD during such visits. Subsequently, the organization comes up with employee schemes both in its HR practices and in setting production targets based on discussion points that arise out of these visits.

There was also the managing director's 'open house' at office. This practice encouraged employees, irrespective of their grades to meet him with their problems, both work related and non-work related, if they feel that they have to meet the MD for an amicable solution. The programme '*I-Speak*' one organization provides an equal opportunity for all its employees to share their concerns from the lowest to the highest level. This is a direct and completely confidential interaction with the Head of Human Resources expressing employees' individual or organizational concerns. Employees can send an e-mail to the Head – Human Resources in complete confidence about anything they wish to speak about. It can include thoughts, ideas, suggestions, views, perceptions, problems, positive feelings and compliments. The promise is that Head Human Resources will get back to them within the next 48 working hours.

Speak Your Mind is the forum and structured device to enable employees seek redressal of grievances that are not covered by the normal ambit of other processes. The objectives are to provide employees with a legitimate platform to ventilate their grievances in strict confidence so as to preserve their morale and motivation; ensure that all employees are treated with justice and fairness without victimization and minimize friction and acrimony to the extent possible so that interpersonal relations are not vitiated. All employees irrespective of grade, location, education, age, sex, etc., can access the grievance redressal scheme. Five organizations studied have Unions that are recognized as the bargaining agent for the workmen in the establishment. All the organizations appear to be in industrial harmony. Majority of them have not had a strike or a lockout for more than a decade now. There are various councils as instruments of dialogue between workers and the management, such as Joint Departmental Council, Joint Consultative Council, Union Management Forum.

4.10 Special Initiatives

One Company collaborated with ILO in the project SAVPOT (South Asia and Vietnam Tripartism and Social Dialogue) from the year 1998 in order to enhance the partnership process with the Union office bearers – who were sent to China and Hong Kong to study the prevailing labour practices and market conditions. Union leaders also attended an ILO delegation at Sri Lanka. In another Organization, once in every three months the Managing Director presents the performance of the organization to the trade union at their union office. Facilitating open communication and transparency, this initiative came from the MD himself. Employee participation in various issues related to decision-making is achieved through the committees. Each Committee is headed by a Senior Manager as Chairman and Union Office bearer as Vice-Chairman. The Committees are safety committee; cultural committee; sports committee; quality committee; community development committee and canteen committee.

4.11 Suggestions for Tatas

In continuation of the tradition built over the years, the *Tatas* need to be trendsetters by framing policies and programmes on the following issues that do not appear to be addressed by the corporates in India:

- Focusing on sexual minorities in the workplace – this involves acknowledging the presence of sexual minorities in the workplace and dealing with them as employees.
- Address sensitive issues such as care for victims of domestic violence amongst their workforce.
- Provide for emerging special groups – the single

parents, persons living with HIV/AIDS, victims of natural disasters and terrorist activities.

- Take the lead in providing job reservations though not necessarily on caste criteria. It could be on the basis of economic backwardness and disabilities.
- Recruit more professional social workers especially in their social initiatives in the permanent rolls of the organizations.
- Provide employment opportunities to the rural youth, following the Titan Industries example, wherever feasible.

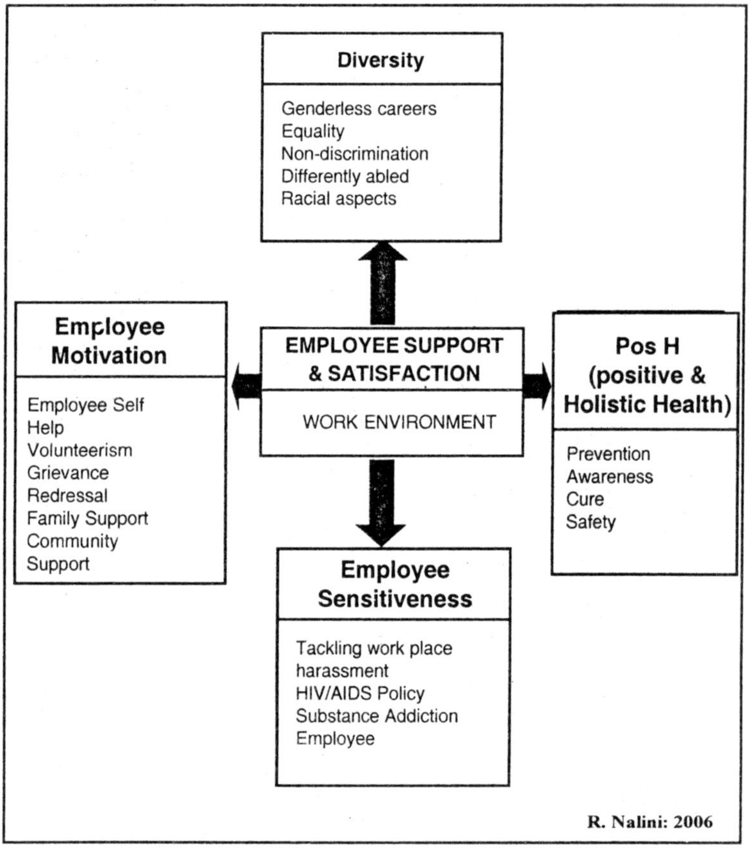

Fig. 4.2 : Towards Promoting Employee Well being & Satisfaction

- Offer employee counselling services in all organizations as a matter of group policy. With stress ever increasing mental health aspects have gained in importance. Keeping in mind Tatas' goal of 'Employee Support and Satisfaction' a model has been suggested in Figure 4.2.

Looking at it from the four facets of diversity, employee motivation, employee sensitiveness and Positive and Holistic Health (PosH), various features such as genderless careers, equality, non-discrimination, prevention, awareness, cure, safety, employee self-help, social work orientation etc. have been included.

The Tatas have pioneered development of employees, community and the nation. They have to a large extent been consistent in their efforts. On an understanding of their established practices, a 'Tata Model on Holistic Development' is presented in Figure 4.3. It is suggested that the industrial organizations implement whatever is feasible to enable effective contribution towards development.

The researcher has attempted to design a model suitable for the country, incorporating the relevant aspects of social work practice in industry by giving a special consideration to the cultural constraints and specifications of Indian conditions.

The idea of designing a model emerged as part of the study but more so with the recent developments occurring in the Indian scenario.In this study model refers to a design that can be used in the industrial organization for the effective implementation of social work practices. Many national and international companies have begun their social initiatives and are likely to establish a potential market. Organizations have begun to recognize the importance of social initiatives, accompanied by an upward movement of NGO sector in India to cater to the needs of the communities/unorganized

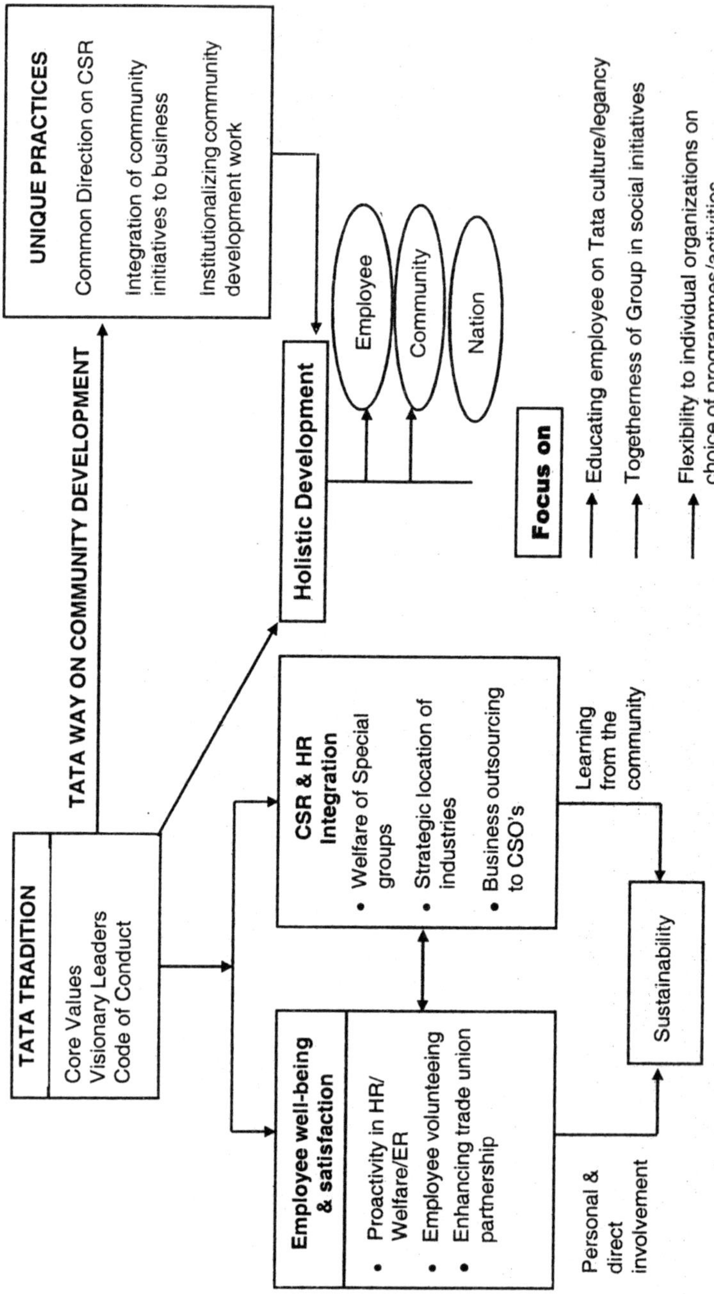

R. Nalini : 2006

Figure 4.3 : Tata Model on Holistic Development

sector workers under different schemes. These are positive signals in the direction of social initiatives becoming an integral part of the world of work.

4.12 Conclusion

This chapter has attempted to understand the various social work practices in the select organizations studied. Classified into HR, welfare, industrial relations and industrial social work, the researcher has described different policies and practices.

5

Social Work Professionals and Practices in the Workplace

5.1. Roles of a Social Worker in the Workplace

A social worker in the workplace has to adorn various roles with corresponding functions, duties and responsibilities as given in the Table 5.1 below. It is essential that the social worker create the opportunity for social work practice.

In all these roles, duty of the social worker is defined as per appointment letter, law and other official documents. Two common responsibilities are inherent for the social worker in all these roles – (a) employee well-being, and (b) orienting all employees and employers in particular about the role, functions, duties and responsibilities of social workers in industry.

This shows that "professional skills equip social workers to function in a variety of human resource programmes" (Berry 1990, Gray & Barrow 1993: 138). Siddiqui & Sukhramani, (2001), described the scenario on field of practice for PSWs in industry in the following words:

> Later the scope of social work professionals expanded to cover industrial relations and personnel management and more recently human resource

Table 5.1 : Social Worker in the workplace: Existence and Expectations

Role	*Function*	*Responsibility*	*Social work component*
Labour Welfare Officer	Providing Statutory/non-statutory welfare measures	Employee Welfare	Need-based, prompt, consistent welfare measures
Industrial/ Occupational Social Worker	Social work interventions with individuals and groups in the organization	Optimum adaptation of individual to the work situation	Application of social work principles and methods in all possible ways at the workplace
Community Development Officer	Organizing and developing the community	Community Development	Use of and innovating with community organization. Capacity building of community
CSR Officer	Implementing the CSR plans of the organization	Coordinate, sustain and develop CSR activities	Ensuring social work principles and methods in all CSR activities
	Counseling of problem employees	Positive mental health of employees	Casework and psychiatric social work for industry
HR Officer	Recruitment to Retirement	Integration of individual goals and organizational goals	Inducting social work at policy level, forming ISW deptt, social work orientation in all HR dealings.
IR Officer	Handling Employee Unions and related matters	Harmonious industrial relations	Orienting line managers, supervisors and employees to constructive disciplining and IR.

management. These social workers are designated as welfare officers, industrial relations officers/ managers, or personnel/human resource managers. Some organizations also employ social workers exclusively to deal with individual employee problems such as absenteeism, drug addiction or alcoholism, etc. This however, is not the predominant mode of social work practice in the Indian context, in the field of work related issues. 'Thus within industrial organizations, a number of trained social

> workers are working but into departments as diverse as labour welfare, personnel, public relations etc.' (Viswanathan, 1963). These professionals perform a variety of functions. There is no consensus among social workers whether all of these are professional social work functions or some are simply managerial functions. (p. 47).

While this debate will remain alive with respect to functions, there is a clear shift of PSWs to other streams within the industrial organizations. PSWs have, largely, shifted from their traditional area of employee welfare to more lucrative areas like human resource management of which employee/ labour welfare is only a part.

5.2.1. Core Functions Handled by Professional Social Workers

Social work practice has been grouped under four major heads: Labour Welfare, Industrial Relations, Human Resources and Industrial Social Work. Accordingly, major responsibilities/functions handled by professional social workers have been grouped into (i) core functions in three major categories as detailed in Table 5.2 and (ii) industrial social work functions, in Table 5.3.

An analysis of data shows that PSWs are engaged in multiple task performance in areas of labour welfare, industrial relations and HR management. Among labour welfare functions, majority is engaged in community work/ corporate social responsibility (50 per cent), implementing welfare programmes (43.18 per cent) and other statutory welfare duties such as housing, canteen, and factory sanitation (36.36 per cent) respectively. In the area of industrial relations, they are engaged in implementing grievance redressal (38.64 per cent), employment standing orders (31.82 per cent), managing unions (36.36 per cent) and discipline matters (34.09 per cent). Training and development

Table 5.2 : Core Functions Handled by Professional Social Workers

Functions (N=88)					
Labour Welfare Functions	*Per cent*	*Industrial Relations Functions*	*Per cent*	*HR Functions*	*Per cent*
Canteen Administration	36.36	Administration of Standing Orders	31.82	Recruitment & Induction	43.18
Factory sanitation and cleanliness	36.36	Works Committee	36.36	Performance Appraisal	47.73
Implementing Welfare Programmes	43.18	Grievance Redressal	38.64	Career Planning	40.91
Recreation	36.36	Handling Trade Unions	36.36	Training & Development	90.91
Housing	36.36	Discipline Matters	34.09	Human Resource Information Systems (HRIS)	19.32
CSR	50.00	Voluntary Retirement	36.36	Exit Interview	38.64

is one of the major areas where an overwhelming majority (90.91 per cent) are involved, followed by basic HR functions like performance appraisal (47.73 per cent) recruitment (43.18 per cent), career planning (40.91 per cent), exit interview (38.64 per cent) and HRIS (19.32 per cent). In a nutshell, most PSWs are performing multiple tasks directly involving the employees.

Navale and Desai (2002) observed that:

> The professional social worker entered the industrial field basically for welfare of the industrial labour and his family, but soon started functioning in other areas too. Implementing various labour legislations as labour officer was the next step. Social worker very well oriented to the agonies of working class, having social work approach is definitely effective in

> implementing labour legislations, justifying his/her place in industry. The social worker equipped with conflict resolutions and conflict management skills and problem-solving approach is best suited to manage the industrial relations functions. A professionally trained social worker with skills in human relations, planning, organizing, evaluating and monitoring is able to carry out functions of Personnel Management with ease and efficiency. Therefore rightly occupies the position of P&A Manager in an organization. Developing potentials of human beings to the maximum possible level is social work objective and social workers are trained well to achieve this objective, which provides them competitive edge to function as Human Resource Developer or as Human Resource Managers. A professionally trained social workers occupying various positions right from trainee to Vice-President (H.R.) in industrial organization practice social work and they stand out with their human touch in their day-to-day functioning. (p. 2).

As Wilk (1988) remarks:

> More and more non-traditional roles are evolving. 'In many companies, the early contracts to provide clinical or single-issue services are broadening. Social workers now work in affirmative action, human resource management, and labour and community relations' (Googins & Godfrey, 1985). Therefore, the sites in the organization where a social worker might work have expanded (p. 223).

5.2.2. Industrial Social Work and PSWs

Industrial social work refers to such social work practices in industrial settings which are rendered by professional social workers to the employees/colleagues or their families. Almost all the professional social workers provide motivation, counselling etc. to the needy employees, irrespective of their position or formal responsibilities. The researcher had asked about their involvement in industrial social work functions directly or indirectly through an open-ended question. The responses are tabulated in Table 5.3.

Table 5.3: Involvement in Industrial Social Work Functions

Industrial Social Work Functions	*Involvement*		
	Direct	*Indirect*	*Undecided*
Individual Employee Welfare	52.27	40.91	6.82
Community Welfare	45.45	47.73	6.82
Policy Formulation	31.82	52.27	15.91
Service Delivery	28.41	36.36	7.95
Employee Counselling	34.09	47.73	18.18

It is interesting to note that most of the PSWs are engaged in some form of activities related to industrial social work. The researcher found that a large number of PSWs directly or indirectly engage themselves in individual employee welfare tasks, community welfare, policy formulation and employee counselling. Though some PSWs admitted that they may not be providing counselling in the strict sense of its definitional and procedural boundaries, yet they do engage in some form such as referral, identification of the problem, motivation etc. To conclude, it could be inferred that majority are performing social work functions in their jobs. The respondents specified that the involvement was at various levels – policy-making, drafting programmes, implementation, evaluation etc. which in turn depended on their positions.

Kurzman and Akbas find (1982):

> Industrial social welfare specialists also occupy – and continue to function as social workers in such varied

> job titles as community development or social responsibility director, equal employment opportunity or affirmative action officer, corporate giving analyst, retiree or education programmes director. If these suggest a broad definition of industrial social welfare specialists, the listing has accomplished its purpose. The criterion that is applied is whether or not the primary focus of the incumbent's activity is within the social welfare arena and makes use of social work expertise (p. 204).

5.2.3 Relevance and Adequacy of Social Work Methods Used

Every profession has certain distinctive values, philosophy, methods and techniques that are imparted to students during the course of their study. Assuming that this specific knowledge could be relevant to the PSWs, the researcher elicited their opinion on the usefulness of various social work methods in the discharge of their duties and responsibilities. Social work has six methods; three basic methods – social casework, social group work and community organization and three auxiliary methods of social welfare administration, social work research and social action.

Table 5.4 : Relevance and Adequacy of Social Work Methods Used

Social Work Methods	*No. of Respondents (N=88)*	*Per cent*
Social Casework	60	68.18
Social Group work	48	54.55
Community Organization	44	50.00
Social Welfare Administration	28	31.82
Social Work Research	26	29.55
Social Action	16	18.18

Social casework is the method frequently used by majority – 68.18 per cent. This is followed by social group work (54.55 per cent) and community organization (50.00 per cent). Social casework and social group work are found to be useful by majority of the social workers irrespective of their specializations. The HR specialists, IR specialists and social work professionals in their core functions are using these two methods quite frequently in executing their duties. HR specialists utilized these two social work methods, in "motivating employees for development". The usefulness of social group work in training and development programmes was also specified by many PSWs.

One IR manager remarked that he has oriented his superiors and line managers to social work approach towards employee discipline. "In the industry, we have to create the opportunity. One needs to explore avenues and set the trend. In my case, I have a social work approach to industrial relations – I believe in the individual's capacity to change. Especially in the case of discipline, my outlook is proactive. I emphasize on self-discipline and assuming responsibility. Lots of programmes are conducted for employees to give them this value addition, making the entire process more productive. If not, the organization will be spending lot of time, energy and money in reacting to discipline. It strains harmonious industrial relations as well". He insisted that in industry, application of social work depended on the individual and his conviction on need for social work in industry. "This again is dependent on the kind of inputs, support and faith on the profession that his institution feeds him with" he said.

The knowledge imparted by social group work helps to address team building, effectiveness and team development since the basic principles of social group work are the core of teamwork. In the IT sector, especially, the nature of work involved emphasizes on group efforts. Toseland and Rivas define group work as a goal-directed activity with small groups of people aimed at meeting socio-emotional needs and accomplishing tasks. This activity is directed to individual members of a group and to the group as a whole within a system of service delivery (Mudgal 1997). However, group work is used by industrial social workers in working on specific groups – alcoholics, diabetic patients, employees with disabled children etc. The social workers in core functions find group work useful in running employee-training programmes and in addressing sensitive issues such as voluntary retirement schemes. One respondent elaborated how the major chunk of group work essentials – group dynamics, group conflict and group management are vital source for training and development programmes.

The third important method of social work is community organization that is being used largely by professional social workers on the field. Five of the Tata organizations studied have a community/social welfare department. PSWs handling department of community welfare or development, family welfare etc. are benefited by the knowledge base of community organization – which they practice in the functional requirements. HR professionals too use this knowledge in framing policies and programmes for community welfare; it also helps them in building relationships and in addressing issues faced by the working community.

Another area, which has benefited from the knowledge of community organization, is the emerging field of corporate social responsibility; social initiatives and promotion of employee volunteering. Partnership programme on areas and issues of social development such as health, education etc. are addressed by PSWs, using community organization as the base – in isolation as well as in integration with other methods. For example, in Titan Industries, the researcher found that their 'Employee Volunteering Programme' on community development initiatives was a tool that enabled employee fulfilment and satisfaction, adding meaning to their lives and also as a tool for job enrichment. While contemplating the relevance of community organization as a method for them, the volunteers argued that the information helped them to function better on the field.

The researcher was told that social workers occupying managerial posts in departments of community welfare or social initiatives etc., find social welfare administration most useful. One respondent who was manager of the family initiatives wing felt that social welfare administration could be applied to "the inevitable administrative work" in fulfilling their duties. For instance, in submitting the annual budget, planning, organizing and coordinating social work initiatives and placing requirements for additional staff members are all made easy because of this method of social work practice.

As far as social work research is concerned, the method has been reported by majority as useful. Social work research is applied in periodic employee surveys on HR practices, organizational climate, job satisfaction etc. As aptly defined by Lal Das (2000) social work research is the application of research methods to the production of knowledge that social workers need to solve problems they confront in their practice. For example, in Tata Tea, before finalizing on the nature of services to be provided to their employees, the organization undertook a research on their needs. The indications were that catering to the disabled children of the employees formed the top priority. It was found that the industrial social worker uses it in obtaining feedback and when introducing new social work initiatives. With respect to social action as a method, only PSWs working for community initiatives have used (14.77 per cent) it but its utility in an organized structure is disputed. A few respondents especially working in HR and IR areas believe that many techniques of social action like lobbying, advocacy etc. are applicable on the job.

The respondents listed the following aspects when asked why they found fieldwork effective: faculty member from the same specialization who had practical knowledge of requirements in the industry; regular industry-institution interaction; objective and periodic feedback on the students' performance; prompt interventions with the agency whenever required; discussions in the individual conferences on common point/extent of meeting of learning objectives and agency's inputs; relevance of placement to the interest of the student; developing interest and conviction to know the role of social work in industry and application of social work methods and techniques (in industry); unbiased, objective and true picture of the agency and agency supervisors' contribution to social work in industry; communicating role expectations from a social work professional in industry; introducing new agencies and withdrawing student placements from those that are not in tune with the learning objectives; periodic group conferences with students from other specializations to know the scope and relevance of social work in the workplace.

5.3 Problems Faced by PSWs

In the third section of this chapter the problems faced by PSWs both in their personal and professional levels are presented. Their self and professional images have also been discussed.

5.3.1 Problems in Executing Job Responsibilities:

Each job has unique characteristics and demands specific qualities from the performer. While social workers are professionally qualified and trained, they too face certain hurdles in performing their jobs. While some of their problems are created by their adjustment with the environment, most of them are by-products of environment and its interaction. Data in this regard is presented in Table 5.6 which shows that a little over one-third PSWs (37.50 per cent) admitted that their problems are initially out of 'mismatch of their training and expectations'. Since industrial organizations are competitive, result producing and fast, the PSWs felt that they have to work under 'pressure to produce quick, tangible, results' (52.27 per cent) in executing their responsibilities, followed by lack of clarity among other colleagues about professional social work (38.64 per cent). A good number of PSWs have reported that they have to work in contradiction to social work ethics (15.90 per cent).

Table 5.5 : Problems Faced in Executing their Responsibilities

Problems	*No. of Respondents (N=88)*	*Per cent*
Having to work in contradiction to social work ethics	14	15.90
Pressure to produce quick, tangible results	46	52.27
Lack of clarity among other colleagues about professional social work principles and practice	34	38.64
Lack of consistency in support from top management	28	31.82
Personal preparedness	14	15.91
Mismatch between training and expectations	33	37.50

Other problems mentioned are the following: scarcity in support from top management according to times/business fortunes; other professional social workers are not very supportive; identity crisis; not being trained in HR aspects; lack of recognition to their course; industrial social work does not seem to grow as a profession and lack of utilization of potential.

The social workers in the workplace are in general victims of ignorance among their colleagues about professional social work practices and methods. Social work *versus* social service is a cliché problem. It surfaces that many do not realize the difference between professional social work and social service, and they thus weaken practice and environment for practice of professional social work. To this inherent problem, the indifference of fellow social workers/academicians adds fuel. The mutual distancing between social work educators and social work practitioners in industry appears to have led to a big gap between theory and practice of social work practice in industry.

The social workers in industry appear professionally isolated. One professionally qualified social worker candidly admitted that, "I am not perceived as a qualified social worker – while I too perceive myself as a hardcore HR professional rather than as a professional social worker practicing HR". The social work institutions have perhaps failed in creating clarity about how professional social workers are constructively different from other HR disciplines. "Having to discover knowledge inadequacies on the job we are frustrated many a times". Social workers in industry admit experiencing this very often. Social work practice all over the country is not adequately documented. There is hardly interaction on social work practice in industry among the practitioners. Thus intricacies and nuances of practices are left to be explored. Practitioners do not have access to such vital information about success and failure stories in social work practice in industry. Moreover, labour welfare officers' induction into industry is as per statutes which have their advantages as well as disadvantages. The welfare officer is not all that welcomed and his status in the organization is disputable. His career growth is limited when compared to core functions of HR that at times result in frustrations.

The grievances of professional social workers are sometimes linked with ethics of social work. Having to work in contradiction of social work ethics sometimes leads even to loss of job. One respondent felt that he had "no scope for applying social work methods and principles because the orientation to URCD at college was totally different from realities. The result based orientation is prevalent in industry whereas we were taught process orientation." However, some that the social workers the researcher interviewed, admitted to have joined Tatas since the Group was known for its social work tradition.

5.3.2 Ethical Issues:

One of the important characteristics of any profession is its ethical base. Most of the professions have written elaborate and approved code of ethics for its fraternity. A few professions have well defined policies, rules and regulations with or without legal sanctions. Therefore the professional bodies regulate their professional behaviours well and also pose disciplinary mechanism and punitive measures for its members. In this study it was found that every sixth respondent (15.90 per cent) has faced problems concerning ethical aspects. A further analysis revealed that issues are wider in nature such as confidentiality, privacy, conflicting interests, contradicting job responsibilities, implementation of written policies etc. There are situations where deviation and dilemmas are found between commitment and action, rhetoric and realities, what is said but not done and what is done but not to be said. Unfair practices have to be made to appear fair with manipulations, tact and skills. If one refuses to be party to such unfair practices, chances of victimization in its various forms are a constant threat. For example, most of the Tata Organizations claim to have history of 'no strike' but only a few concerned persons know that behind such situations are carefully worked out plans and counter plans to thwart a movement. The rights of employees for formation of union or concerted action are curbed. As noted by Bahl (1995):

> The TISCO management was aware of the advantages resulting from its welfare activities for the workers. In a report prepared by TISCO on the medical service provided in the welfare work at Sakchi, it was noted: it must however be said that British and American experience points to the

> probability that the expenditure incurred on welfare work, even when undertaken wholly or primarily from purely humanitarian or philanthropic motives, is very quickly remunerative, and in the long run actually profitable to the firm or company providing it. The advance in efficiency of the operatives, their improvement in *physiques* and *morals*, the greater stability of the whole staff, and the consequent saving in recruiting and replacement – together with the *intangible results of increased loyalty to the interests of the employer*, and of an intensified *esprit de corps* – are believed to overweigh in sheer money gain, the whole cost of the welfare work undertaken. (p. 123-124).

5.3.3 Problems in Career Growth

Every individual needs recognition for his work. Accordingly one should be moving upward vertically in the career ladder. Many PSWs in the industry have restricted opportunities for career growth. As mentioned earlier, industrial organizations are providing opportunities for PSWs of different specializations with varied opportunities. In table 5.7 the point of entry of PSWs specialization-wise, growth opportunities and career best are given below:

Thus, the role of a social worker in industry is largely determined by the position he or she occupies. A social worker has various posts to enter, occupy and grow but the number of positions is limited and also not exclusive. PSWs have to face stiff competition from other disciplines.

The researcher found that in one organization the career growth for PSWs was virtually absent. The PSWs had joined as labour welfare officers and had remained there. These welfare officers are in the 'staff category'. This is a grade that covers the clerical staff and hence these welfare officers are not management staff. They have been designated as welfare officers, placed in the staff category that is third 'rung' in the

Table 5.6: Opportunities for Social Workers in the Workplace

Entry	*Specialization*	*Growth*	*Career Best*	*Nature of Appointment*
Labour welfare officer/HR trainee/ Management Trainee	PMIR/HR	Various managerial positions in HR/Indust-rial Relations	Head of the Organization, HR/IR departments, Training & Development Division etc.	As regular employees in the rolls of the organization
Counsellors, industrial social wor-ker, labour welfare officer	·MPSW/ FCW	Permanency of post, inde-pendence in functioning, recognition for the func-tion, acce-ssibility and acceptance across hier-archy levels	Head of the Department, increasing the size and scope of the department	Project basis, consultant, retainer, part time basis apart from regular, full time basis
Community Development Officer, Community Initiatives Officer, CSR Officer, labour welfare officer	URCD	Permanency of post, independence in functioning, recognition for the func-tion, accessibility and acceptance across hierarchy levels	Head of the Department, increasing the size and scope of the department	Project basis, consultant, retainer, part time basis apart from regular, full time basis

hierarchy ladder and continue to stay there for more than 8 years now – on an average. They are not unionized either. The management has not so far drafted a career path for these welfare officers. The concern for these officers is the threat that they may reach retirement in the same grade. The welfare officers do get a yearly increment based on their performance assessment. The increment is as per the salary structure and benefits as applicable to the organization. They feel that only when the professional social workers shift tracks to Human Resources (HR) or Industrial Relations (IR) do they get into the mainstream functions and appropriate career leaning. Earlier their team was bigger with more than eighteen welfare officers. Many of them had left after understanding their low opportunities for career growth. Those who are continuing in the organization appear demotivated. Many questions arise – are they justified in aspiring for a career considering they are professional social workers? Is position important in the hierarchy to deliver goods? The welfare officers agreed that they do not want to join and retire as welfare officers– their career stagnation is a matter of serious concern. The researcher felt that perhaps the problem is inherent in the profession itself. Drawing a career path for a professional social worker in industry, one finds that from labour welfare officer he or she has to enter mainstream functions of HR for progress. Exclusive labour welfare or industrial social work does not guarantee professional advancement and where it does, it is rather slow or limited. The social work institutions should prepare their students accordingly. To prevent disillusionment on the job, social work educators have a moral responsibility to highlight to the students what awaits them in their work front.

Multi-skilling is inevitable in the industrial organizations and it happens with social work professionals as well. The researcher found Heads of HR who have started their career in the community development wing of the company. Similarly there was one professional social worker, who, after putting in nearly nine years of service in the HR department, was holding the post of community development head. The researcher infers that such type of job rotations or multi-skilling is not welcomed generally by the social workers. While shift from community development wing to the HR though a parallel/lateral one in the organizational hierarchy is considered a positive move for better career options, the *vice versa*, as discussion suggests, is not so positively perceived.

As mentioned above, career orientation among social workers is another question that has not been fittingly answered. The researcher feels that problems arise when social workers compromise on their professional ethics for the sake of career growth. This phenomenon, however, is not unique only to the industrial setting.

The latest trend is that many social workers are entering industry as consultants/retainers but not as permanent employees of the organizations. Departments that are delivering services on a regular basis, such as community development and corporate social responsibility activities had its appointments made on contractual or project basis. The researcher came across instances where professional social workers were working as consultants for Tata. What was surprising was that, even freshers from social work institutions were being designated as consultants. In another organization, a team of three social workers, all fresh post-graduates were found working in the CSR project on a contract basis. This growing trend of contractual appointment is neither good for the young professionals nor for the organization. The researcher infers that this practice is in a bid to avoid payment of benefits a permanent employee would be entitled to; even more glaring is the threat to the future of social workers in Tatas in such areas of work. Being trend setters and leaders in the field of social initiatives, the Tatas have an ethical responsibility in such aspects too.

It appears that when a professional social worker occupies a policy-making position his scope for traditional social work practice decreases. However, it also appears that a PSW at a higher level inducts more of his professional fraternity apart from bringing in his knowledge base. The researcher found that the PSWs heading social initiatives wing of their organization too have performed well, expanded their base and created more space for their fellow professionals.

5.3.4 Problems in Updating Knowledge

Knowledge enrichment through constant upgradation is one of the cornerstones of the knowledge society in the post globalization era. Do PSWs use this opportunity to update themselves and if not what problems do they face – these were some of the questions raised with them. Contrary to beliefs, it was found that there are opportunities but not many PSWs are able to enjoy the same because of varied reasons like workload, inadequate number of staff members and lesser space for research and innovation. They also said that their knowledge is updated mainly through in-house interaction, access to the internet and by being in touch with PSW friend in the non-industrial setting. Finally, the subject of insufficiency in updating knowledge is a genuine problem, which could create other impasse – no satisfaction, feeling of becoming obsolete, a sense of boredom and monotony.

PSWs also brought to focus the other side to the issue of knowledge upgradation. They are sources of data to be explored on field based knowledge, experiential learning, success and failure stories that need to be documented. This documentation will be a valuable source of knowledge for the students of social work. The PSWs regretted the fact that none of the social work institutions have ever sincerely attempted to do so. One respondent was very happy that the researcher has taken the initiative to understanding PSWs in industry and commented, "this is a very relevant study". All these reiterate the need for mutual exchange of knowledge and updating to enable a healthy 'Industry-Institution Interface'.

Social work is the youngest of all human service professions and its orientation, scope and operation have undergone changes consistently in line with the changes in the society. Subsequently, social work education has also responded to these changes as when the need arose. As stated by Desai, (2001):

> During the first decade of social work education (1936-46), the focus was on social sciences, social problems and social policies. In mid-fifties, focus shifted to method approach and casework was given prime attention, group work was next in popularity and community was the least. In 1970, the thrust came on developmental issues and therapeutic / welfare social work remain no longer the only concern of social work. (p. 316).

As observed by Bhatt, (2006), in the post-globalization period, social work profession is responding to issues at the micro and macro levels; it has equal priority for interpersonal, intrapersonal concerns, special groups and community problems. Workplace has been one such area of practice where the scope for social work practice has grown in the last two decades.

Respondents felt that faith in the development of people makes one realize that social work is possible irrespective of settings. Employees are a community and they also need help of social workers. "Employees accept me as humane mainly because of my social work approach to the HR profession. It helps me view individuals as whole persons. I am able to create confidence in people to solve their problems themselves". One respondent had listed out the following five Cs as vital for professionals in practice of social work methods and principles in industry. Conviction – the passion to innovate and initiate social work in the workplace; Competency – thorough subject knowledge and skills; Contemplation – deliberations into feasibility and suitability;

Consistency – of efforts and Courage – to withstand pressures. To sum up, PSWs are able to use their knowledge and practice their knowledge consciously.

5.4.1 Scope for Social Work Practice

The question that was raised to the PSWs was on their perspective on the broad areas of social work practice.

Table 5.7 : Broad Areas of Social Work Practice

Areas	*No. of Respondents (N=88)*	*Per cent*
Employee Welfare and Life Services	46	52.27
Disability Management	31	35.23
Developing Individuals	57	64.77
HRD	36	40.91
Employee Relations	47	53.41
Transitions and Change	59	67.05
Crisis Management	49	55.68
Privacy Concerns	23	26.14
Welfare of Special Groups	19	21.59

The data highlights the fact that majority (67.05 per cent) felt that dealing with transitions and change in their organization as an area of social work practice. This change could be in job contents, early separation schemes, attitude towards recovered clients etc. The PSW has a crucial role to play in such instances arising out of transition and change.

Hanson (1993), remarked:

> The reintegration of clients into the workplace is essential to support their recovery. Organizational factors, such as drinking cultures, occupational stresses, and supervisory biases, may precipitate relapse. In addition, many supervisors and co-workers do not recognize the seriousness of substance abuse or the fact that recovery continues when employees return to work. Therefore, it is important that if the client's permission can be obtained, social workers attempt to prepare organizational members for the return of the recovering employees. Meetings with managers, supervisors and union representa-

> tives can alert them to particular problems that recovering employees encounter and can enlist their support. The creation of support groups for recovering substance abusers can provide additional assistance. (p. 226).

Apart from the above, the changes in the nature of work happening rampantly have to be addressed.

Morgan (1988) observed:

> To this is the added stress of the change or elimination of many jobs. Individuals have to be helped to separate their self-concept from their work position. With the prospect of several career changes in a lifetime, individuals must be helped to adapt, to let go, and grasp a new identity in a new field. Social workers can help provide the support to the person while making the transition. A new sense of self-identity is necessary, one is apart from that given by the job. Individuals need to see that all is not lost if they can no longer make steel or no longer teach. I hope that the social workers can understand this need for job adaptability and can be helpful. Understanding the forces of change is an essential prerequisite to helping. (p. 342).

Another significant area of social work practice, which has been mentioned by a good majority is developing individual employees including training and development, organizational behaviour and leadership.

Crisis response is an area of social work practice for more than half the PSWs. Crisis intervention is a method for actively influencing psychosocial functioning during a period of disequilibrium. Human service professionals have been attracted to crisis intervention as a promising and apparently effective method of delivering rapid services (Parad 1988). Providing for employee welfare and life services comes next.

Core HRD was mentioned as an area by 40.91 per cent PSWs. PSWs see employee welfare and life services as an area for social work intervention. One-third PSWs (35.23 per cent) specifically pointed out disability management and one fifth (21.59 per cent) mentioned that welfare of the special groups at the workplace offered avenues for social work skills.

As described by Akabas & Gates (1993):

> The components of a disability management programmes include the following: Conducting a needs assessment; appointing a coordinating committee; developing policies and procedures; designating a case manager; establishing mechanisms for early case finding; providing transitional and accommodated employment options; offering training to those with new, programmes-related responsibilities; setting up a data collection and evaluation method and preventing disability. Many of these roles can be carried out by social workers who have some connections with the world of work. Other social workers can be partners in efforts that involve other workplace actors. (p. 245).

Interestingly 26.14 per cent said that privacy concerns of the employees (clients) were handled effectively due to social work knowledge.

5.4.2 Relevance of Social Work in the Workplace

Since the debate on whether social work is relevant in industrial organizations or not has gained importance in the post-globalization period, this question was posed to the PSWs. In fact, PSWs are posed with the challenge of continuously proving the relevance of social work in the workplace. The relevance of social work professionals are less challenged by other professionals rather than their own.

As Thomlison (1983) noted:

> Industrial social work is a collaborative endeavour and issues of employee care must be resolved through interdisciplinary communication, cooperation and

> respect for each profession's expertise. In this regard the industrial social worker brings a knowledge of interpersonal relations, counselling skills and community resources which significantly add to the workplace resources. (p. 23).

It is important for social workers in the workplace to understand that employees are their prime focus.

Kurzman (1988) commented:

> Occupational social work expertise is not in promoting profit maximization but in helping organizations meet the needs of the individuals, groups and communities in the world of work – and, reciprocally in recognizing unions' and managements' obligation and vested interest in doing so. We are specialists in the human dimension of the workplace and in increasing our labour and industrial sponsors' commitment of both human and fiscal resources in this arena. Such clarity about our role and function is essential to ensure that people will be the central focus of our attention; that a goal will be to enhance the quality of life for workforce participants; and that our commitment will be both to the provision of social services and to the creation of humanistic forms of organizational change. (p. 21-22).

Table 5.8 : Relevance of Social Work in the Workplace

Perceptions	*No. of Respondents (N=88)*	*Per cent*
Relevance		
Yes	84	95.45
No	04	4.55
Reasons		
Human side is not to be neglected	64	72.73
Production is dependent on people	42	47.73
Employee as groups have specific problems	53	60.23
Specific problems need specific professional intervention	56	63.64
Fast changing nature of human/ organizational problems	68	77.27
Responding to time and place	14	15.91

An over whelming majority (95.45 per cent) has pointed out the relevance of social work in the workplace in a positive way and the rest (4.55 per cent) have not found any relevance. PSWs have specified various reasons to prove their point but two prominent arguments in favour of its relevance were: changing nature of human / organizational problems (77.27 per cent) and the impossibility of neglecting human side of an enterprise (72.73 per cent). The next two arguments are interrelated: employees in an organization have specific problems (60.23 per cent) and specific problems require specific professional intervention (63.64 per cent). Nearly half of them have also mentioned that production takes place due to people not because of machines alone (47.73 per cent). One respondent said, "social work is relevant in the workplace because of its human element and its uniqueness in facing situations and solving problems".

Winkelpleck & Smith (1988) observed:

> Wrich (1980) indicates that 10 per cent to 12 per cent of the workforce has serious personal problems. Each person who has experienced a serious personal problem knows the dramatic influence such problems have on attitudes and behaviour at work. Although exact rates of deterioration range dramatically, a 15 per cent deterioration rate is commonly expected. Imagine that 10 per cent of the people with whom you work today are only performing at 85 per cent capacity. More painfully, imagine the emotional cost to these employees, to their co-workers, and to their families as the impaired job performance becomes more blatant. The early signs of potential impaired performance are subtle. (p. 45).

In such situations, social work not only cures, but also prevents problems from manifesting through appropriate interventions.

Wilks *et al.* (1988) wrote:

> Social workers are trained to approach clients in a holistic manner, seeing the person as a multi-levelled, multi-faceted organism with biological, psychological and social characteristics, needs and problems. Therefore, a social worker may be ideally suited to serve in coordinative and integrative capacities, both during the planning stage or programmes and when they are actually implemented. Also, those social workers who have training in occupational settings are likely to appreciate the importance of securing the support and assistance of manages and to have the skills necessary to gain that support. Additionally, social workers' training provides them with knowledge both about human behaviour in its biological, psychological, and social aspects, and about the range of community services and resources. (p. 209).

5.4.3 Prospects for Social Work in the Workplace

The functions/roles of social workers can be categorized into two: (i) basic social work functions; and (ii) allied social work functions. In the category of basic social work functions one can place all such functions that are most acceptable to any social work professional such as counselling, welfare, community services, CSR, EAP etc. whereas functions related to personnel, administration, training and development, employee relations, HRD Practices, organizational behaviour, organizational development etc. can be placed under the category of allied social work functions. Even those who are against social work in workplace have no objection if a social work professional is engaged in performing basic social work functions. All such functions are considered by them as professional setting whereas allied social work function may be denoted as non-professional setting.

As also noted by Kernaghan (1983):

> An increasing number of social workers have contracted employment in non-professional settings; most notably in industry. We now find ourselves in a milieu where rules of privacy are not always practiced in the way we have known or understood them. Dialogue is more often than not with non-professionals who are not bound by our codes of ethics and whose interests are, appropriately, more aligned with business than the social and health issues. Although the significant relationship between these seemingly diverse interests have been recognized and has resulted in the increasing employment of social workers, nurses and psychologists in industry. It is nevertheless important that such professionals review and clarify their roles and responsibilities. (p. 39).

While the debate whether industry is any more an area of professional social work practice will remain alive, it will not be out of place that the academic distinction of basic *versus* allied functions is not acceptable to practicing social work professionals in the workplace. This also counters the basic principles of specialized invention, extension of knowledge and in disciplinarian nature of any profession. Against this backdrop, the PSWs were asked about their roles in the workplace. Table 5.10 contains the responses:

Table 5.9 : Role of social worker in the workplace

Roles	*Responses (N=88)*	
	PSWs	*Per cent*
To manage specialized social services	36	40.91
To provide professional services like counselling	38	43.18
To promote industrial relations	60	68.18
To promote HRD	68	77.27
To work on labour welfare	42	47.73
To work with the community in and around the plant	44	50.00

An overwhelming majority (77.27 per cent) felt that the role of the social worker in the workplace is to promote Human Resource Development (HRD); while 68.18 per cent felt that their role is to promote industrial relations. While 50 per cent of the PSWs felt that their role lies in working with the community in and around the workplace; 47.72 per cent felt it was labour welfare; 43.18 per cent felt their role was to provide professional services like counselling and 40.91 per cent identified their role in managing specialized services. Some respondents mentioned other roles of social worker in the workplace as: ability to assess the risk and diagnose from human element point of view and advise workplace on the future aspects; help the employee in any genuine situation; to work with the absolutely non-working community residing in the periphery; to carry on the regular HR functions and apply the social work knowledge to the extent of its relevance; to ensure high satisfaction and motivation among employees; integrate CSR with normal business processes and to document what exactly happens in the social work practice and process in the workplace.

Saxena (2004) rightly described:

> Social work professionals play a very important role of a catalyst in the inculcation of values and skills and attitudes. Social work professionals working as human resource experts and personnel managers guide and nurture the employees' right from recruitment, induction to their advancement in the organization. They act as enabler, guide and help the individuals to solve their problems and function to their full potential. (p. 1).

Some respondents have said that in the Information Technology (IT) sector the application of social work is different and hence the role of social worker would differ too. It all depends on the nature of social work practice in the workplace.

The role performance of any professional is governed by a number of factors as well as synergetic and interactive reinforcement between various components of a sub -system in an organization.

5.4.4 PSWs on Social Work Training

Bargal, (2000) says that occupational social workers are in an excellent position to effect change because of their proximity to both management and workers. They may contribute towards shaping the new industrial organizational reality and lowering the human cost of economic changes. However, in order to effectively achieve this goal they will have to improve their professional training, develop a more scholarly culture, and attain an integrative and influential position in new workplaces emerging in the 21st century.

As Antoniades & Belllinger (1983) put it,

> Although the field of social work is in a state of flux, as exemplified by the number of new and traditional roles social workers now play in a variety of settings, there is a fundamental value system that the profession adheres which should hold it in good stead wherever the profession is practiced. What will assist them to function in the most positive way is their adherence to social work values. (p. 33).

PSWs felt that: social work teaches the principle of controlled emotional involvement that helps in dealing with human beings; internalizing social work principles/values, helps in building high emotional intelligence; in crisis intervention; social work is very relevant to human beings; social work inculcates a strong belief in the individual's capacity to change that is very useful in dealing with human element of the organization; it gives insight into problems individuals carry to workplace and how the 'whole person' theory operates; it teaches how to be issue based in functioning – the key to dealing with people in HR field; it helps in easy communication with people, in relating to their needs, problems and aspirations; it teaches to solve the community's problems scientifically; helps bring about development approach in community development activities; offers maximum self-development through understanding problems and people; it produces open, mature and confident individuals; understanding oneself, the work situation, colleagues, their needs and problems keeps increasing because of social work education and outlook; able to know individual strengths and weaknesses in functioning; equipped with understanding of human behaviour and its causative factors one develops the aptitude to anticipate problems and tackle them accordingly; gives the required confidence in handling human and interpersonal relations; helps to treat every single person as unique individual with some capacities to perform certain roles; understanding of individuals and group behaviour; social work enables a humane approach to employee issues and not viewing them as economic tools; develops a positive outlook to life and helps in accepting the individual with his problems and shortcomings. The PSWs' reasons for relevance of social work training in the workplace are capsuled (see figure 5.2).

An overwhelming majority of 95.45 per cent feels that social work in workplace should continue to be part of the social work curriculum. This could be due to its relevance, scope and usefulness on the job and their strategic position in the organization. The PSWs expressed the need for continuing social work in workplace aimed at providing person-environment fit in a variety of situations. "It means utilizing the knowledge and skills accumulated over the last several decades of social work practice in the workplace and the scholarly work associated with it and applying them to other settings" (Iverson, 1998 quoted by Mor Barak 2000: 205).

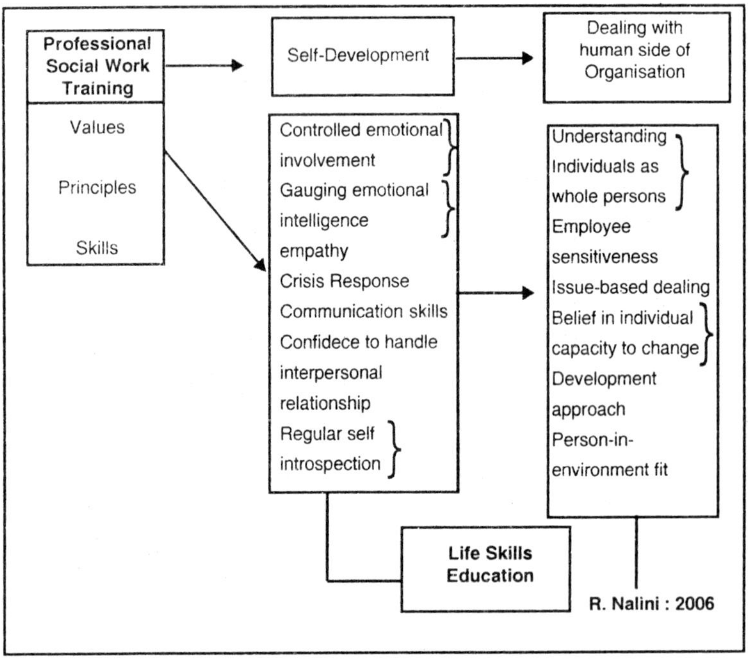

Fig. 5.1 : Relevance of Social Work Tranning in the Workplace

Table 5.10 : Continuance of Social Work in the Workplace in the Curriculum

Continuing social work in industry in curriculum	*No. of Respondents*	*Per cent*
Yes	84	95.45
No	04	4.55
Total	88	100

With corporate social responsibility emerging as a key area, the social workers are equipped to bring a new direction to the CSR activities of the organization.

Smith (1988) reflects:

> Few corporate leaders understand the dynamics of human service delivery at the community as well as social workers do. Likewise, few organizational

> leaders have the time or the training to identify and prioritize local social welfare needs. Social workers have contributed time and talent to specific community projects or trained and then evaluated organizational volunteers in the latters' attempts to improve the quality of life in their respective communities. (p. 13).

5.4.5 Will Social Work Survive in the Workplace?

Due to the changing business processes it is heading in the path of extinction. In the rapidly changing economic environment, would social work as a profession be able to sustain itself and survive? This question was put forth to the PSWs. The PSWs irrespective of their area of operation unanimously responded highlighting its strengths and enriched the researcher with their insights.

As reiterated by Kurzman (1993):

> Despite the changing workplace and the changing nature of work itself, individuals and families continue to depend on work and the workplace even more than before because other social systems – such as the church, school, political club, ethnic organization and local community – may be functioning less extensively or effectively than in the past. Therefore, the challenge to occupational social work may be conceptualized as resulting from the need to respond at the workplace to some of the unmet needs of workers and their families. Providing social services, influencing policies on human resources and moving towards the individual (and collective) empowerment of workers and work organizations are roles that are compatible with both the profession's ideology and practice. (p. 388).

Table 5.11 : Future of Social Work in Industry

Future	*No. of Respondents*	*Per cent*
Bright	60	68.18
Gloomy	16	18.18
Unpredictable	12	13.64
Total	88	100

A majority (68.18 per cent) says that the future of social work practice in industry is bright. 18.18 per cent say it is gloomy and 13.6 of them are undecided. This shows that the future is bright but competitive as well.

As elaborated by Barak (2000):

> Traditionally, occupational social work covered "policies and practices targeted at workers, under the sponsoring auspices of trade unions and employers, that are available at the workplace or in the community, to individuals whose eligibility results from their status as workers or their dependent relationship to employers" (Akabas, 1993, p. xviii). The workplace and the organization of work in our society are changing dramatically and the implications of these changes for the workforce are far reaching. In order to provide services to populations in need, it may be time for occupational social work to redefine its parameters and include all aspects of work, *regardless of the auspices under which occupational social work is practiced.* (p. 201).

Corporate social responsibility has become an important part of mostly all leading business ventures in India. It is true not only for promoting itself amongst its external customers, but also the internal ones – the employees.

Social work in the workplace, in the future is bound to face lot of challenges and demands for innovative practices. Smith (1988) appositely described:

> The future is figuratively bright with challenges and opportunities. Social workers are problem-solvers and change agents. That's how we make our living. That's how we enjoy so much of our professional lives. It should be obvious that the workplace is simply too rich in opportunities for professional reward and service to people for it to be abandoned. A task that lies before social workers is that of exploiting to the fullest the possibilities we have in order to serve humankind in the natural lifespace of work. (p. 348).

5.5 Conclusion

The professional social worker has to ensure that the human element of the enterprise is happy both as an individual and as an employee. His roles, functions and duties are his instruments towards achieving this end. The social work professionals have a variety of fields to choose from in the workplace.

Bibliography

Abraham, P.F. (2004). Employee Assistance Programme (EAP): An emerging area of social work practice in India. *Social Work Review*, special issue, 61-75.

Abramovitz, M., & Epstein, I. (1983). The politics of privatization: Industrial social work and private enterprise. *The Urban and Social Change Review*, 16 (1), 13-19.

Acharya, T. L. (1953). Philosophies of labour welfare. *The Indian Journal of Social Work*, 14 (1), 41-44.

Ahluwalia, G. S. (1953). Philosophies of labour welfare. *The Indian Journal of Social Work*, 14 (1), 50-54.

Ahuja, R. (2001). *Research methods*. New Delhi: Rawat Publications.

Akabas, S. H. (1978). Fieldwork in industrial settings: Opportunities, rewards, and dilemmas. *Journal of Education for Social Work*, 14 (3), 13-19.

Akabas, S.H. (1982). The world of work: A site for mental health promotion. In Felice, P. (Ed.), *New direction for mental health services: Mental health promotion and primary prevention*. (pp.112).San Francisco: Jossey-Bass.

Akabas, S. H. (1984). Workers are parents, too. *Child Welfare*, 63 (5), 387-399.

Akabas, S.H. (1995). Occupational social work. In R. Edwards (Ed.), *Encyclopedia of Social Work*, 19th edition, Silver Spring, MD: NASW.

Akabas, S.H., & Farrell, B.G. (1993a). Prevention: An organizing concept for workplace services. In Kurzman, P.A., & Akabas, S.H. (Eds.), *Work and well-being: The occupational social work advantage.* (pp.86-101). Washington, DC: NASW.

Akabas, S.H., & Gates, B.L. (1993b). Managing disability in the workplace: A role for social workers. In P.A., & Akabas, S.H. (Eds.), *Work and well-being: The occupational social work advantage.* (pp.239-255). Washington, DC: NASW.

Akabas. S.H., & Gates, B. L. (2000). A social work role: Employment equity for people with serious and persistent mental illness. In Mor Barak, M. E., & Bargal, D (Eds.), *Social Services in the workplace: Repositioning occupational social work in the new millennium.* (pp. 163-184). New York, USA. The Haworth Press.

Akabas, S.H., Kurzman, P.A., & Kolben, N.S. (1979). (Eds.), *Labour and industrial settings: Sites for social work practice.* New York: Columbia University, Hunter College & Council on social work education.

Akabas, S.H., & Kurzman, P.A. (1981). Industrial social work as an arena for practice. *Social work,* 26, 52-59.

Akabas, S.H., & Kurzman, P.A. (1982a). The industrial social welfare specialist: What's so special? In Akabas, S.H., & Kurzman, P.A. (Eds.), *Work, workers, and work organizations: A view from social work.* (pp.197-235). Englewood Cliffs, NJ: Prentice Hall.

Akabas, S.H., Kurzman, P.A. (1982b), (Eds.), *Work, workers and work organizations: A view from social work.* Englewood Cliffs, NJ: Prentice-Hall.

Akabas, S.H., & Akabas, S.A. (1982c). Social services at the workplace: New resource for management. *Management Review,* 71, 15-20.

Akabas, S.H. (1983). Industrial social work: Influencing the system at the workplace. In M. Dinerman (Ed.), *Social Work in a turbulent world.* (pp.224). Silver Spring: NASW.

Akabas, S.H., & Kurzman, P.A. (1993). (Eds.), *Work and well-being: The occupational social work advantage.* Washington DC: NASW.

Andrew, W. (1975). A social service strategy in industry. *Social work,* 20, 402.

Anthony, P.D. (1984). *The ideology of work.* London: Tavistock Publications.

Antoniades, R., & Bellinger, S. (1983). Organised worksites: A help or hindrance in the delivery of social work services in and to the workplace? In R.J. Thomlison (Ed.), *Perspectives on industrial social work practice.* (pp.29-38). Ottawa: Family Service Canada.

Antony, D. (2004). *Human resource development practices and their impact on organizational effectiveness: A study of selected industrial organizations.* Ph.D. Thesis. Department of Commerce, University of Delhi.

Asch, A., & Abelson, P. (1993). Serving workers through managed health care: The social work role. In Kurzman, P.A., & Akabas, S.H. (Eds.), *Work and well-being: The occupational social work advantage.* (pp.123-137). Washington, DC: NASW.

Badhani, K.N. (1992). *Corporate social accounting in public enterprises in India.* Ph.D. Thesis, Department of Commerce, Kumaun University Campus.

Bagali, M.M., & Joshi, S.S. (2001). Occupational social work in industry: A way. *Indian Journal of Social Research,* 37(2), 149-153.

Bakalinksy R., (1980). People *vs.* profits: Social work in industry. *Social Work,* 25, 471-475.

Balgopal, P. R., De Silva, E., Mun, L. W. & Choo, Q. A. (1997). Improving quality of work life in Singapore: Implications for social work in industries. *Employee Assistance Quarterly*, 12 (4), 51-60.

Bargal, D. & Karger, Howard, J. (1991). Occupational social work and the new global economy. *Administration in Social Work*, 15 (4), 95-109.

Bargal, D. (1993). An international perspective on the development of social work in the workplace. In Kurzman, P.A., & Akabas, S.H. (Eds.), *Work and well-being: The occupational social work advantage*. (pp.372-385). Washington, DC: NASW.

Bargal, D. (2000). The future development of occupational social work. In Mor-Barak, M.E., & Bargal, D. (Eds.), *Social Services in the Workplace: Repositioning occupational social work in the new millennium*. (pp. 139-156). New York, USA: The Haworth Press.

Basu, K.S. (1953). Philosophies of labour welfare. *The Indian Journal of Social Work*, 14(1), 58-59.

Benedict, S.D. (1973). A generalist counsellor in industry. *Personnel and Guidance Journal*. 51, 717-722.

Berkowitz, M. (1962). Social workers in Indian industry. *Social Service Review*, 36 (4), 412-420.

Bhandarkar, P.L. (1977). *A sociological study of minority community: Case Study of the PARSIS of Nagpur*. Ph.D. Thesis, Department of Sociology, Nagpur University.

Bhatt, S. (1991). Indian trade unionism: Challenges in coming decade. *Haryana Labour Journal*, 22 (3), 12-14.

Bhatt, S. (2001). Occupational social work in India: Opportunities and challenges. *Contemporary Social Work*, 18, 33-51.

Bhatt, S. (2005). Occupational social work as a field of social work practice. In Singh, S., & Srivatsava, S.P. (Eds.) *Teaching and practice of social work in India: Realities and responses*. (pp. 235-247). Lucknow: New Royal Company.

Bhatt, S., & Abraham, P.F. (2005). *Corporate social responsibility: An area of occupational social work practice.* Paper presented in the national seminar on Voluntary Initiative of NGO and Corporate Sector for Social Development: Issues and Challenges, Faculty of Social Work, M.S. University, Baroda.

Bhatt, S., & Nalini, R. (2005). *Convergence of HRD and voluntary initiatives for corporate social responsibility: A case study of Titan Industries Limited, Hosur.* Paper presented in the national seminar on Voluntary Initiative of NGO and Corporate Sector for Social Development: Issues and Challenges, Faculty of Social Work, M.S. University, Baroda.

Bhatt, S., & Sharma, R. (2005). Public-private partnership for rural development. *Contemporary Social Work,* 22, 13-25.

Brand, S. H., & Yasser, R. (1977). Social Work in Industry. In Sobie, F. (Ed.), *Changing roles in social work practice.* Philadelphia: Temple University Press.

Brilliant, E.L., & Rice, K.A. (1988). Influemeny corporate philanthropy. In Gould, G.M., & Smith, M.L. (Eds.), *Social work in the workplace: Practice and principles.* (pp.299-313). New York: Springer Publishıng Company, Inc.

Brisebois, R.M. (1983). Victim assistance: An example of meeting the work related needs of employees. In Thomlison, R. J. (Ed.), *Perspectives on industrial social work practice.* (pp. 123-132). Canada: Family Service Canada Publications.

Brown, J.A.C. (1954). *The social psychology of industry.* Great Britain: Penguin Books.

Carroll, A, B. (1999). Corporate social responsibility: Evolution of a definitional construct. *Business and Society,* 38 (3), 268-295.

Carter, I. (1977). Social work in industry: A history and a viewpoint. *Social Thought,* 3 (1), 7-17.

Ceccarelli, F. (1986). *The industrial sociologist as a manager in a work organization*. USA: American Sociological Association (ASA).

Chatterjee, N.R. (1969). *A study of some psychological problems of middle level executives in selected large industrial undertaking in India*. Ph.D. Thesis, Department of Psychology, University of Delhi.

Choi, S. (2003). Roles and opportunities for social work intervention in expatriate work environments. *International Social Work*, 46 (2), 221-233.

Chandler, R. G., Kroeker, B. J., Fynn, M., & MacDonald, D. A. (1988). Establishing and evaluating an industrial social work programme: The Seagram, Amherstburg experience. *Employee Assistance Quarterly*, 3 (3-4), 243-253.

Cherin, D. A. (2000). Organizational engagement and managing moments of maximum leverage: New roles for social workers in organizations. In Mor Barak, M. E., & Bargal, D. (Eds.), *Social Services in the Workplace: Repositioning occupational social work in the new millennium*. (pp. 29-46). New York, USA: The Haworth Press.

Chinappan, M.V. (1995). *A study of relationship between organizational culture and employee commitment*. Ph.D. Thesis, Department of Social Work, Tata Institute of Social Sciences.

Cook, P., & Terruso, R. (1983). An industrial social service delivery system at the crossroads: The case of District Council 37, American Federation of State, County and Municipal employees. In Thomlison, R. (Ed.), *Perspectives on industrial social work practice*. (pp. 111-122). Canada: Family Service Canada Publications.

Cooke, W.P. (1985). Industrial social work: Direct and indirect services and consultation. In Arthur E.F., Jane H.P., & Andrew W.D. (Eds.), *Fields of social work*. (pp.377-385). USA: Sage Publications.

Corwin, D.M. (1993). Solution-focused brief workplace counselling. In Kurzman, P.A., & Akabas, S.H. (Eds.), *Work and well-being: The occupational social work advantage.* (pp.200-217). Washington, DC: NASW.

Coulshed, V., & Mullender, A. (2001). *Management and social work.* New York, USA: Palgrave Publishers.

Crump, Larry. (1987). The economic sector of Japanese society: An exploration for social welfare activities. *International Social Work,* 30 (4), 343-351.

Csiernik, R. (1998). An integrated model of occupational assistance. *The Social Worker,* 66 (3), 37-47.

Cunningham, G. (1990). Social work and employee assistance programmes: Emerging issues. *Social Thought,* 16 (1), 34-40.

Daniel, C.J. (1983). Industrial social work: A human relations process. *Personnel Today,* 3 (4), 20.

Daniel, L. Jr. (1981). Industrial social work: Into the computer age. *EAP Digest,* 1, 19.

Das, P., & Merchant, D. (1982) .The social worker in Indian industry. *Business India,* 86-90.

Datt, R., & Sundharam, K.P.M. (2005). *Indian economy.* New Delhi: S. Chand & Company Limited.

Davis, G. (1985). Retooling: Clinical social worker to occupational social worker. *Social Case Work,* 66, 498-503.

Dawson, S. E. (1993). Social work practice and technological disasters: The Navajo Uranium experience. *Journal of Sociology and Social Welfare,* 20 (2), 5-20.

Denzin, N. K. (1995). Living and dying in an employee assistance program. *Journal of Drug Issues,* 25 (2), Spring, 363-378.

Desai, A. B. (2000). *Social work practice in industry: Study of gaps as perceived by professional social workers between actual and ideal practice.* Ph.D. Thesis, Department of Social Work, M.S. University.

Desai, A.B., & Raijada, S. (2005). University-industry interface a paradigm shift from process to result orientation – an HR education: Study camp experience. *Social Work Review*, special issue, 150-155.

Desai, M. (1991). Issues concerning the setting up of social work specializations in India. *International Social Work*, 34 (1), 83-94.

Desai, M. (2002). *Ideologies and social work: Historical and contemporary analyses*. New Delhi: Rawat Publications.

Desai, M.M. (1971). Industrial social work in retrospect. *The Indian Journal of Social Work*. 31(4), 431-433.

Desai, M.M., & Dole, V. (1979). *Industrial Social Work*. Mumbai: Tata Institute of Social Sciences.

Dhingra, O.P. (1964). Counselling services for industrial workers. *Social Work Forum*, 2 (2), 15-19.

Dhumale, A.G. (1982). *A study of the managements' perception of the workers' problems and the role of a social worker in Indian industry*. Department of Social Work, Tata Institute of Social Sciences.

Edwards, S. T. (1953). Philosophies of labour welfare. *The Indian Journal of Social Work*, 14 (1), 44-50.

Faul, A. C. (2002). Comprehensive assessment in occupational social work: The development and validation of the corporate behavioural wellness inventory. *Research on Social Work Practice*, 12 (1), 47-70.

Filipowicz, A.C. (1979). The troubled employee: Whose responsibility? *The Personnel Administrator*, 24, 19.

Fleming, C.W. (1979). Does Social Work Have a Future in Industry? *Social Work*, 24, 183-185.

Frank, R., & Streeter, C. L. (1985). Identifying roles for social workers in industrial settings: A multi-level conceptual framework. *Social Work Papers*, 19, 14-22.

Fredenhagen, H. (1961). Function of personnel social work. *International Social Work*, 4, 31-35.

Frenkel, S. J. (1986). Industrial sociology and workplace relations in advanced capitalist societies. *International Journal of Comparative Sociology*, 27 (1-2), 69-86.

Freund, A. (2005). Work attitudes of social workers across three sectors of welfare organizations: Public, for-profit, and third sector. *Journal of Social Service Research*, 31 (3), 69-92.

Fricke, E., & Fricke, W. (1977). Industrial sociology and the humanization of work. *Soziale Welt*, 28 (1-2), 91-108.

Friedlander, W.A. (1970). Labour unions and social workers. *International Social Work*, 13(4), 28-31.

Gajendragad, J. (2004). Counselling in industries: Critical issues and implications. *Social Work Review*, special issue, 114-119.

Gal, J., & Bargal, D. (2002). Critical junctures, labour movements and the development of occupational welfare in Israel. *Social Problems*, 49 (3), 432-454.

Gallie, D. (1989). From industrial sociology to the sociology of work: A review of English research since the 1960s. *Sociologia del Lavoro*, 35-36, 15-34. Gambrill, E., & Pruger, R. (Eds.), (2001). *Controversial issues in social work*. Berkeley: University of California.

Gavin, J. F., & Maynard, William, S. (1975). Perceptions of corporate social responsibility. *Personnel Psychology*, 28 (3), 377-387.

Goldbeck, W. B. (1988). AIDS and the workplace: Business fights the epidemic. *The Futurist*, 22 (2), 18-19.

Goel, S.L., & Jain, R. K. (1988). *Social welfare administration*. New Delhi: Deep & Deep Publications.

Googins, B. (1975). Employee assistance programmes. *Social Work*, 20, 464-465.

Googins, B. (1987a). *Occupational social work: A bibliography*. Washington DC: NASW.

Googins, B. (1987b). Occupational social work: A developmental perspective. *Employee Assistance Quarterly*, 2 (3), 37-53.

Googins, B. (1993). Work-site research: challenges and opportunities for Social work. In Akabas, H. S., & Kurzman, P. A. (Eds.), *Work and well-being: The occupational social work advantage.* (pp.61-78). Washington DC: NASW

Googins, B., & Godfrey, J. (1985). The evolution of occupational social work. *Social Work*, 30, 396-402.

Googins, B., & Godfrey J. (1987). *Occupational social work.* Englewood Cliffs, NJ: Prentice Hall.

Gokhale, R. G. (1953). Study of prevailing practices. *The Indian Journal of Social Work*, 1953, 14, (1), 6-63.

Gonzalez P., & Jose Manuel. (1984). Marx and industrial sociology. *Revista Internacional de Sociologia*, 42-50, 361-404.

Gore, M.S. (1997). A historical perspective of the social work profession. *The Indian Journal of Social Work*, 58(3), 442-455.

Goss, S., & Mearns, D. (1997). Applied pluralism in the evaluation of employee counselling. *British Journal of Guidance and Counselling*, 25 (3), 327-344.

Gould, M. G., & Smith, L. M. (1988). *Social Work in the work place: Practice and Principles.* New York: Springer Publishing Company, Inc.

Gray, M., & Barrow, F. (1993). Ethnic, cultural, and racial diversity in the workplace. In Kurzman, P.A., & Akabas, S.H. (Eds.), *Work and well-being: The occupational social work advantage.* (pp.138-152). Washington, DC: NASW.

Gribas, J., Vik, P., & Christensen, J. (2003). The impact of supervisor influence strategy and relational context on readiness to change for the alcohol abusing employee. *Employee Assistance Quarterly*, 19 (2), 1-17.

Gustavsson, N. S., & Balgopal, P. R. (1991). Training of social workers in work settings: Response of the academia. *Employee Assistance Quarterly*, 6 (4), 79-89.

Hall, LaCheata & Others. (1991). Likelihood to use employee assistance programs: The effects of socio-demographic, social-psychological, socio-cultural, organizational, and community factors. *Journal of Employment Counselling*, 28 (2), 63-73.

Hans, B.C.S. (1974). *Not for work alone: Services at the workplace.* NewYork: Urban Research Center, Hunter College.

Hansen, S. (2004). From 'common observation' to behavioural risk management: Workplace surveillance and employee assistance, 1914-2003. *International Sociology*, 19 (2), 151-171.

Hanson, M. (1993). Serving the substance abuser in the workplace. In Kurzman, P.A., & Akabas, S.H. (Eds.), *Work and well-being: The occupational social work advantage.* (pp.218-238). Washington, DC: NASW.

Hanlan, A., & Jocobs, S. (1969). Social work and private industry. *Social Casework*, 50 (3), 152-156.

Harlow, K. C. (1998). Employee attitudes toward an internal employee assistance programme. *Journal of Employment Counselling*, 35 (3), 141-150.

Harris, J.J. (1993). Military social work as occupational practice. In Kurzman, P.A., & Akabas, S.H. (Eds.), *Work and well-being: The occupational social work advantage.* (pp.276-290). Washington, DC: NASW.

Hasenfeld, Y. (2000). Social services and welfare to work: Prospects for the social work profession. In Mor Barak, M. E., & Bargal, D. (Eds.) *Social Services in the workplace: Repositioning occupational social work in the new millennium.* (pp. 185-200). New York, USA: The Haworth Press.

Hatia, O. P. (1969). The personified image of personnel officers in India. *The Indian Journal of Social Work*, 30 (2), 157-164.

Healy, Karen. (2004). Social workers in the new human services marketplace: Trends, challenges and responses. *Australian Social Work*, 57 (2), 103-114.

Herzberg, F. (1965). The new industrial psychology. *Industrial and Labour Relations Review*, 18 (3), 364-376.

Hoffer, A. (1989). Educational ingredients for occupational social work practice. *Journal of Social Work Education*, 25 (3), 212-223.

Hodson, R. (1985). Working in "high-tech": Research issues and opportunities for the industrial sociologist. *The Sociological Quarterly*, 26 (3), 351-364.

Highhouse, S. (1999). The brief history of personnel counselling in industrial-organizational psychology. *Journal of Vocational Behaviour*; 55 (3) 318-336.

Hughes, E. C. (1957). The relation of industrial to general sociology. *Sociology and Social Research*, 41 (4), 251-256.

Hughes, C. (1976). Making unions unnecessary. New York: Executive Enterprises Publications Co., Inc.

Ilavarasan, P. V., & Sharma, A. K. (2001). Software work in India – Routinisation or post-modernization. *Guru Nanak Journal of Sociology*, 22 (2), 1-25.

Iversen, R. R. (1998). Occupational social work for the 21st century. *Social Work*,43 (6), 551-566.

Jacob, K.K. (1970). *Personnel management in India: A study of training and functions of personnel officers*. Ph.D. Thesis, Udaipur School of Social Work, Rajasthan Vidyapeeth.

Jacob, K.K. (1973). *Personnel Management in India: A study of training and functions of personnel officers*. Udaipur: SJC Publications.

Jacob, K.K. (ed.), (1987a). Silver Jubilee Special on Social Work in Industry. *Rajasthan Journal of Social Work*, Rajasthan Vidyapeeth.

Jacob, K.K. (1987b). *Industrial Social Welfare*. Encyclopedia of social work in India, 2, 105-113.

Jacob, K.K. (2004). Social work in industry: Issues, strategies and challenges. *Social Work Review*, special issue, 1-8.

Jacob, K.K. (2005). Social work and H.R.D.: Uniqueness and commonness. *Social Work Review*, special issue, 11-24.

Jacobson, J. M. (2004). Compassion fatigue among employee assistance programme counsellors. *Dissertation Abstracts International, A: The Humanities and Social Sciences*, 65 (4), 1540-A.

Jain, S. (1988). *Sexual equality: Workers in an Asian plantation system*. Bangalore, India: Sterling Publishers Private Limited.

James, P. (2000). Human resources development: A social work perspective. *Indian Journal of Training and Development*, 30(4), 33-43.

James, T.W. (1974). *The Employee assistance programme*. Center city, Minn: Hazelden Foundation Books.

Jhingon, Uma. (1953). *Welfare activities for the TATA employees of the TISCO Ltd., Jamshedpur*. M. A. Project, Department of Social Work, University of Delhi.

Ji, Gopal. (1979). *Personnel management in Indian industries*. Ph.D. Thesis, Department of Commerce, University of Delhi.

Jocelyn, S. (1980). Open letter from a social worker in a private industry. *Australian Social Work*, 33, 47-48.

Johnson, P.R., & Gardner, S. (1999). Domestic violence in the workplace: Developing a company response. *Journal of Management Development*, 18(7), 590-597.

Joseph, C. (1978). *The personnel officer in industrial relations: A sociological study*. Ph.D. Thesis, Department of Sociology, University of Delhi.

Kamatchi, P. (2003). *A study on corporate social performance with special reference to ethical issues in marketing*. Ph.D. Thesis, Department of Commerce, University of Bangalore.

Kanhere, V.S. (1982). *White collar unionism: A sociological study of officers' associations in nationalized banks in Ahmedabad.* Ph.D. Thesis, Department of Sociology, University of Gujarat.

Karkare, S. (2005). HR intervention in quality management system: A G.TEK experiment. *Social Work Review,* special issue, 133-136.

Kern, B., Kern, H., & Schumann, M. (1988). Industrial sociology as catharsis. *Soziale Welt,* 39 (1), 86-96

Kernaghan. C. P. (1983). Privacy in industry: A professional position. In Thomlison, R.J. (Ed.), *Perspectives on industrial social work practice.* (pp. 39-46). Canada: Family Service Canada Publications.

Khan, G.C., & Sinha, D. (2001). Developing employee assistance programme in industry: Challenging priority in the 21st century. *Perspectives of Social Work,* 16(3), 15-21.

Khasgiwala, A., & Bulchandani, A. (2005). Human resource challenges in health sector with special reference to hospital system. *Social Work Review,* special issue, 117-125.

Khasgiwala, A., & Navale, A. (2004). (Eds.) Special issue on Social work in industry. *Social Work Review.* Vadodara: Faculty of Social Work, M.S. University.

Khasgiwala, A., & Navale, A. (2005). (Eds.) Special issue on Social work and human resource education. *Social Work Review.* Vadodara: Faculty of Social Work, M.S. University.

Knudsen, H. K., Roman, P. M., & Johnson, J. A. (2003). Organizational compatibility and workplace drug testing: Modelling the adoption of innovative social control practices. *Sociological Forum,* 18 (4), 621-640

Kochar, K. V. (1960). Applied social sciences in industry. *The Indian Journal of Social Work,* 21 (1), 39-46.

Klein, L. (1976). *A social scientist in industry*. Essex: Bowker Publishing Company Ltd.

Kudchedkar, L.S. (1966). From labour welfare to personnel management. *The Indian Journal of Social Work*, 27 (1), 1-6.

Kudchedkar, L.S. (1979). *Aspects of personnel management and industrial relations*. New Delhi: Tata McGraw Publishing Company Limited.

Kulpinska, J. (1968). Industrial sociology in Great Britain: Theory and practice. *Przeglad Socjologiczny*, 22 (1), 107-114.

Kumar, S. (1981). Relevance of social work education for welfare officers. *Indian Worker*, 21 (47), 67-69.

Kurzman, P. A. (1983). Ethical issues in industrial social work practice. *Social Casework*, 64,105-111.

Kurzman, P.A. (1993). Employee assistance programmes: Towards a comprehensive service model. In Kurzman, P.A., & Akabas, S.H. (Eds.), *Work and well-being: The occupational social work advantage*. (pp.26-45). Washington, DC: NASW.

Kurzman, P.A. (1993a). Work-site research: Challenges and opportunities for social work. In Kurzman, P.A., & Akabas, S.H. (Eds.), *Work and well-being: The occupational social work advantage*. (pp.61-78). Washington, DC: NASW.

Kurzman, P. A. (2000). Bakalinsky's conundrum: Should social workers practice in the world of work? In Mor Barak, M. E., & Bargal, D. (Eds.), *Social Services in the workplace: Repositioning occupational social work in the new millennium*. (pp. 157-162). New York, USA: The Haworth Press.

Lala, R.M. (1993). *Beyond the last blue mountain: A life of J.R.D. TATA (1904-1993)*. New Delhi: Penguin Books India (P.) Limited.

Lala, R.M. (1995). *The joy of achievement: Conversations with J.R.D.TATA*. New Delhi: Penguin Books India (P.) Ltd.

Lala, R.M. (1998). *The heart beat of a trust*. New Delhi: Tata McGraw Hill Publishing Company Limited.

Lal Das, D. K. (2000). *Practice of social research*. Jaipur & New Delhi: Rawat Publications.

Langensee, G. (1970). Social Work in German Industrial Enterprise. *Social Work Forum*, 8(1), 20-26.

Lawrence, J. A., Boxer, P., & Tarakeshwar, N. (2002). Determining demand for EAP services. *Employee Assistance Quarterly*, 18 (1), 1-15

Lebowitz, M. M., Zischka, P. C., Mahon, M., & McCarley, L. D. (1982). Issues in macro-level industrial social work practice. *Administration in Social Work*, 6 (2-3), 139-146.

Legáz, L. (1958). The trade union as a social group. *Revista Internacional de Sociologia*, 15 (58), 221-237.

Leicht, T.K. & Fennell, L.M. (2001). *Professional work: A sociological approach*. Great Britain: Blackwell Publishers.

Leighninger, L. (2000). When social workers and unions allied in the 1930s. *Journal of Progressive Human Services*, 11 (2), 103-112.

Leiter, M. P., & Wahlen, J. (1996). The role of employee assistance counsellors in addressing organizational problems. *Employee Assistance Quarterly*, 12 (1), 15-28

Leijnse, F. (1978). The practical use of social research by trade unionism. *Mens en Onderneming*, 32 (2-3), 160-170.

Lonne, B., McDonald, C., & Fox, T. (2004). Ethical practice in the contemporary human services. *Journal of Social Work*, 4 (3), 345-367.

Lowry, C. E., Paul, S. C., Morrill, W. H., & Oviatt, B. E. (1987). Examining person and environment variables related to work performance, work satisfaction, and psychological adjustment: Preparation for preventive interventions. *Social Work Papers*, 20, 54-66.

Lynch, J. (1983). Labour-Management issues: The Interlock experience. In Thomlison, R.J. (Ed.), *Perspectives on industrial social work practice*. (pp. 73-82). Canada: Family Service Canada Publications.

Maanen, J.V. (Ed.). *Qualitative Methodology*. New Delhi: Sage Publications.

MacEwen, Sally. (1983). Training and orientation in the workplace. In Thomlison, R.J. (Ed.), *Perspectives on industrial social work practice*. (pp. 67-72). Canada: Family Service Canada Publications.

Mackay, Lesley. (1981). Industrial sociology: Who wants to know? *The Sociological Review*, 29 (2), 253-270.

Madonia, J. F. (1983). Approaches to social work field placements in industry. *Journal of Education for Social Work*, 19 (3), 38-47.

Madonia, J. F. (1985). Handling emotional problems in business and industry. *Social Casework*, 66 (10), 587-593.

Madhukar, M. (1976). *A study of the managements' perception of the workers' problems and role of social workers*. Department of Social Work, Tata Institute of Social Sciences.

Magaret, A., & Wendy, B. (2003). *Research for social workers: An introduction to methods*. Jaipur: Rawat Publications.

Maiden, R. P. (1987). Ethical issues in occupational social work: Implications for practice. *The Journal of Independent Social Work*, 1 (4), 31-40.

Maiden, R. P. (1992). First world EAPs serving third world clients: A U.S. perspective of the South African experience. *Employee Assistance Quarterly*, 7 (3), 1-15.

Mani, P.M., & Anish, K.R. (2004). Industrial mental health: A social work perspective. *Social Work Review*, special issue, 76-84.

Mamkoottam, K. (1977). *Politics of trade unions: A case study in Jamshedpur*. Ph.D. Thesis, Department of Sociology, University of Delhi, Delhi.

Mannheim, B., & Papo, E. (2000). Differences in organizational commitment and its correlates among professional and non-professional occupational welfare officers. In Barak, M. E. M., & Bargal, D. (Eds.), *Social Services in the workplace: Repositioning occupational social work in the new millennium*. (pp. 119-138). New York, USA: The Haworth Press.

Marlow, C. (1991). Occupational social work and employee assistance programmes in Great Britain. *Employee Assistance Quarterly*, 7 (1), 19-24.

Masi, A.D., & Reisch, M. (2001). Should social workers work for for-profit firms? In Gambrill E., & Pruger, R. (Eds.), *Controversial issues in social work*. (pp.27-38). Berkeley: University of California.

Masi, D.A. (1982). *Human Services in Industry*. Lexington, MA: Lexington Books.

Masi, F. A., & Spencer, G. E. (1977). Alcoholism and employee assistance programmes in industry: A new frontier for social work. *Social Thought*, 3 (1), 19-27.

Mathew, P.M. (1967). Social worker in industrial organization. *Social Work Forum*, 5(4), 7-12.

Mathew, P.M. (1972). *Social worker in industrial organization: Readings in personnel management*. New Delhi: Orient Longman Publishing Company.

McCarthy, D. E. & Steck, S. B. (1989). Social work in private industry: Assessing the corporate culture. *Employee Assistance Quarterly*, 5 (1), 19-35.

Mclean, J., & Andrew, T. (2000). Commitment, satisfaction, stress and control among social service managers and social workers in the UK. In Barak, M. E. M., & Bargal, D. (Eds.), *Social Services in the workplace: Repositioning occupational social work in the new millennium*. (pp. 93-118).

New York, USA: The Haworth Press.

McCorquodale, B. (1983). The view from the family service association board level. In Thomlison, R. (Ed.), *Perspectives on industrial social work practice*. (pp. 57-66). Canada: Family Service Canada Publications.

McCroskey, J., & Scharlach, A. (1993). Family and work: Trends and prospects for dependent care. In Kurzman, P.A., & Akabas, S.H. (Eds.), *Work and well-being: The occupational social work advantage*. (pp.153-169). Washington, DC: NASW.

McGregor, D. (1960). *The human side of enterprise*. Bombay: Tata McGraw-Hill Publishing Company.

McGilly, F. (1985). American historical antecedents to industrial social work. *Social Work Papers*, 19, 1-13.

Mehta, B. (2005). Introducing social work concerns related to women among future HR managers: An effort through fieldwork learnings. *Social Work Review*, special issues, 74-78.

Mehta, M., & Gill, S. (2005). Emerging roles of HR professionals in changing corporate environment. *Social Work Review*, special issue, 79-88.

Menon, J. (1974). *A study of workers' problems and the role of social worker in industry* of Social Work, Tata Institute of Social Sciences.

Merhotra, G.N. (1975). *Studies in industrial sociology: The Indian context*. Lucknow: Atma Ram & Sons.

Miley, K.K., O'Melia, M., & DuBois, B.L. (1995). *Generalist social work practice: An empowering approach*. Needham Heights, Massachusetts: A Simon & Schuster Company.

Miller, S. (2001). *Social action: A teleological account*. United Kingdom: Cambridge University Press.

Mishra, L. (2001). *Economy and labour*. New Delhi: Manak Publications Private Limited.

Mishra, J.P. (2004). Corporate social responsibility. *Social Work Review*, special issue, 37-42.

Misra, S. (1990). Personnel management function and education in a changing environment. *The Indian Journal of Social Work*, 51 (2), 243-259.

Molley, D.J., & Kurzman, P.A. (1993). Practice with unions: Collaborating toward an empowerment model. In Kurzman, P.A., & Akabas, S.H. (Eds.), *Work and well-being: The occupational social work advantage*. (pp.46-60). Washington, DC: NASW.

Monappa, A. (1997). *Managing human resources*. New Delhi: Macmillan India Limited.

Mor-Barak, M.E. (2000b). Repositioning occupational social work in the new millennium. In Mor-Barak, M.E., & Bargal, D. (Eds.), *Social Services in the workplace: Repositioning occupational social work in the new millennium*. (pp. 201-211). New York, USA: The Haworth Press.

Mor-Barak, M. E., Poverny, L. M., Finch, W. A. Jr., McCroskey, J., Nedelman, H. L., Seck, E. T., & Sullivan, R. (1993). A model curriculum for occupational social work. *Journal of Social Work Education*, 29 (1), 63-77.

Mor-Barak, M.E. & Tyman, Margaret. (1993). Older workers and the workplace: A new challenge for occupational social work. *Social Work*, 38 (1), 45-55.

Mor-Barak, M.E., & Bargal, D. (2000a). Human services in the context of work: Evolving and innovative roles for occupational social work. *Administration in Social Work*, 23 (3-4), 1-11.

Mor-Barak, M.E., & Bargal, D. (2000b). Human services in the context of work: Evolving and Innovative roles for occupational social work. In Mor-Barak, M.E., & Bargal, D. (Eds.), *Social Services in the workplace: Repositioning occupational social work in the new millennium*. (pp. 1-11). New York, USA: The Haworth Press.

Mor -Barak, E. M., & Bargal, D. (Eds.), (2000c). *Social services in the workplace: Repositioning occupational social work in the new millennium*. New York: The Haworth Press, Inc.

Mor-Barak, M.E., Findler, L., & Wind, L.H. (2003). Cross-cultural aspects of diversity and well-being in the workplace: An international perspective. *Journal of Social Work Research and Evaluation*, 4 (2), 145-169.

Morton, T. D. (1981). Organizational development as a variant of community development. *Social Development Issues*, 5 (2-3), 90-98.

Moses, Dorothy. (1950). Social work in industry. *Indian Journal of Social Work*, 11(1), 76.

Moxley, D. P. (2002). Social work strategies and tactics in the workplace: Socialization of people with disabilities. *Journal of Social Work in Disability and Rehabilitation*, 1(3), 43-60.

Mudgal, S. D. (1997). *An introduction to social work*. Jaipur: Book Enclave.

Mudrick, N. R. (1991). An underdeveloped role for occupational social work: Facilitating the employment of people with disabilities. *Social Work*, 36 (6), 490-495.

Murthy, S. A. S. (1953). Absenteeism in industry. *The Indian Journal of Social Work*, 14 (2), 132-143.

Murthy, B. S., & Patro, G. C. (1977). Social responsibilities of industry: A study of the Belpahar experiment. *The Indian Journal of Social Work*, 37 (4), 343-355.

Nagar, B. (2004). Industry and social work. *Social Work Review*, special issue, 50-52.

Naidu, Y. (2005). Corporate Social Responsibility (CSR) in India: Interventions on HIV / AIDS. *Perspectives in Social Work*, 20(1), 18.

Nadkarni, L. (1998). *Sociology of industrial worker*. Jaipur: Rawat Publications.

Naik, A. K., & Das, G. N. (2002). A study on the nature of job, absenteeism and labour turnover in coal industry of Jharsuguda District of Orissa. *Guru Nanak Journal of Sociology*, 23 (2), 39-49.

Nair, R. (2003, December 3rd). The human element. *Hindustan Times*, .H1.

Nalini, R. (2004). Industrial social work for employee development: A case study. *Social Work Review*, special issue, 107-113.

Nalini, R. (2005). Social work and industry in India. In Singh, S., & Srivatsava, S.P. (Eds.) *Teaching and practice of social work in India: Realities and responses*. (pp. 255-266). Lucknow: New Royal Company.

Navale, A., & Desai, A. (2002). *Reviewing social work education in industry for remodelling social work education*. Paper presented at the National Seminar on Social work education: Realities and Responses. Organized by D.S.A., Departments of Social Work, Delhi University, Jamia Milia Islamia and Lucknow University, 7-9 November, 2002.

Navale, S.A., Vyas, M.D., & Sharma, M. (2004). Changing profile of industry: Social work response. *Social Work Review*, special issue, 93-101.

Navale, S.A., Vyas, M.D., & Sharma, M. (2005). Use of indigenous literature and research in HR education: Roles of schools of social work. *Social Work Review*, special issue, 126-132.

Nazimova, A. K., & Cherkasov, C. N. (1974). The sociological service at an industrial enterprise. *Sotsiologicheskie Issledovaniya*, 1 (1), 117-126.

Newman, R. P. (1983). Programme evaluation as a reflection of programme goals. In Thomlison, R. (Ed.), *Perspectives on industrial social work practice*. (pp. 83-110). Canada: Family Service Canada Publications.

NITIE Alumini Association. (1988). *Social View of Industrial Relations*. Mumbai: Jaico Publishing House.

Orii, H., & Kenzo, O. (1958). *Management and Workers: An example of human relation management in an enterprise*. Tokyo: Diamond Company.

Oxley, G. B. (1969). Industrial social work in Peru: A descriptive study. *Social Service Review*, 43 (1), 59-68.

Ozawa, M. (1980). Development of social services in industry: Why and how? *Social Work*, 464-469.

Ozawa, M. N. (1983). Social work practice in Employee Assistance Programmes. *Social Casework*, 64, 243-246.

Pandey, S.N. (1989). *Human side of TATA Steel*. New Delhi: TATA McGraw Hill Publishing Company Limited.

Pandey, S.N. (1991). *Social side of TATA Steel*. New Delhi: TATA McGraw Hill Publishing Company Limited.

Panwalkar, V.G. (1989). *Organizational effectiveness for resource mobilization: An assessment of a rural development project sponsored by an industry*. Ph.D. Thesis, Department of Social Work, Tata Institute of Social Sciences.

Parmar, M.N. (2005). Organizational effectiveness and empirical effectiveness, prime HR value addition factors: Social work perspective. *Social Work Review*, special issue, 100-116.

Patel, C. (2001). Indigenizing social work education: A case study from Baroda. *The Indian Journal of Social Work*, 62(2), 197-218.

Pathak, N.S. (2005). Health and stress. *Social Work Review*, special issue, 31-43.

Paul, R. (1977). *Dimensions of current research in occupational alcoholism*. New Orleans: Mimeo, Tulane University.

Paul, R. M. (1987). EAP: Issues for social work practice. *Social Casework*, 68, 503-506.

Pawar, M. (1999). Professional social work in India: Some

issues and strategies. *The Indian Journal of Social Work*, 60(4), 566-586.

Peterson, D. K. (2004). The relationship between perceptions of corporate citizenship and organizational commitment. *Business and Society*, 43 (3), 296-319.

Pertzoff, L. (1979). An alcoholism programme in an industrial setting. *Smith College Studies in Social Work*, 49 (3), 209-228.

Pinto, S. (1984). *Education and industrial productivity: A case study of workers employed in the engineering industry in Pune metropolitan region*. Ph.D. Thesis, Indian Institute of Education, Pune.

Popp, J. R. (2003). *Power and stigmatization in self-referral to employee assistance programmes: Does race/ethnicity or gender matter?* Sociological Society (SSS), Conference paper.

Popple, P. R. (1981). Social work practice in business and industry, 1875-1930. *Social Service Review*, 55 (2), 257-269.

Poverny, L.M. (2000a). Employee assistance practice with sexual minorities. In Mor-Barak, M. E., & Bargal, D. (Eds.), *Social Services in the workplace: Repositioning occupational social work in the new millennium*. (pp. 69-92). New York, USA: The Haworth Press.

Poverny, L. M. (2000b). Employee assistance practice with sexual minorities. *Administration in Social Work*, 23, (3-4), 69-91.

Powell, D. F. (1957). Recent trends in industrial sociology. *American Catholic Sociological Review*, 18 (3), 194-204.

Preparatory Asian Regional Conference. (1947). Labour in India. Delhi: International Labour Organization.

Pushpanandham, K. (2005). Total quality people management: A strategy for people management in organizations. *Social Work Review*, special issue, 137-144.

Radovanovic, M. (1971). The industrial sociologist and the

conflict between humanistic and management requirements of profession and social practice. *Socioloski Pregled*, 5 (1), 18-29.

Raber, M. J., & Conrads, A. P. (1999). Distributive justice in the workplace: Emerging social work interventions. *Social Thought*, 19 (1), 15-28.

Rajendran, K., Rao, V. N., & Reddy, M. V. (1997). A study on occupational stresses and coping patterns in an industry. *NIMHANS Journal*, 15 (3), 233-241.

Ram, E. J. S. (1950). Social work in industry. *The Indian Journal of Social Work*, 11, (1), 80-85.

Ram, E. J. S. (1953). Study of prevailing practices. *The Indian Journal of Social Work*, 14, (1), 63-69

Ramanathan, C.S., & Ramakrishnan, K.R. (1987). Industrial alcoholism and social work intervention. *Management and Labour Studies*, 12, 1-7.

Ramanathan, C.S. (1989). Review of strategies for employee assistance programmes: The crucial balance. *Management and Labour Studies*, 14 (2), 120-121.

Ramanathan, C. S. (1990a). Stress and job satisfaction: Implications for occupational social work. *Employee Assistance Quarterly*, 6 (2), 27-39.

Ramanathan, C.S. (1990b). Employee assistance programmes: Past, present and future. In Ferris, J., Rowland, K., & Buckley, M.R. (Eds.), *Human resources management: Perspectives and Issues*. Boston: Allyn and Bacon.

Ramanathan, C.S. (1992). EAPs response to personal response and productivity: Implications for occupational social work. *Social Work*, 37, 234-239.

Randeria, K.N. (1963). Personnel management and social work. *Indian Journal of Social Work*, 24(2), 132.

Rao, A.V.R. (1965). *Industrial social services in a developing economy*. Madras: Allied Publishers Private Limited.

Rawat, B.D. (1988). *Labour welfarism in India*. Jaipur: R B S A Publishers.

Report of the Tata Council for Community Initiatives. (2001). Mumbai: Tata Services Limited.

Reddy S.C. (1996), Industrial social work. *HRD Newsletter*, 9-10

Reichert, Elisabeth. (2003). Workplace mobbing: A new frontier for the social work profession. *The International Journal of Continuing Social Work Education*, 5 (3), 4-12.

Resnick, H., & King J. (1985) Shadow Consultation: Intervention in industry. *Social Work*, 30, 447-450.

Rex, A. S., Daniel B., & Otto F. J. (1974). Social work practice in industry. *Social Work*, 19, 280-287.

Rim, Y. (1977). Significance of work and personality. *Journal of Occupational Psychology*, 50 (2), 135-138.

Robert, J. (1974). Industrial social work in context: Points and view points. *Social Work*, 19, 655-656.

Robbins, P. S. (1997). Organizational Behaviour. New Delhi: Prentice Hall of India Private Limited.

Robbins, P. S., & Sanghi, S. (2005). *Organizational behaviour*. Delhi: Pearson Education (Singapore) Pvt. Ltd.

Root, S. L. (1999). Social work and the workplace. In Reisch, M., & Gumbrill, E. (Eds.), *Social work in the 21st century*. California: Pine Forge Press.

Root, L. S. (2000). Education and training in the workplace: Social work interventions in the private sector. *Administration in Social Work*, 23 (3-4), 13-28.

Root, L.S. (1993a). Employee benefits: The role of social insurance and social services. In Kurzman, P.A., & Akabas, S.H. (Eds.), *Work and well-being: The occupational social work advantage*. (pp.102-122). Washington, DC: NASW.

Root, L.S. (1993b). Unemployment and underemployment:

A policy and programme-development perspective. In Kurzman, P.A., & Akabas, S.H. (Eds.), *Work and well-being: The occupational social work advantage*. (pp.332-349). Washington, DC: NASW.

Rubin, A., & Babbie, E. (2001). *Research methods for social work*. California: Brooks/Cole Publishing Company.

Saini, R. (1970). Social work in industry. *Social Work Forum*, 8(1), 16-10.

Saini, R. (1971). Social work management objectives. *The Indian Journal of Social Work*, 31(4), 435-438.

Saltzberg, M., & Bryant, C. (1988). Family systems theory and practice at the workplace. *Social Work Papers*, 21, 16-27.

Salvi, P.M. (2000). *The role of social support in effective implementation of office automation*. Ph.D. Thesis, Department of Personnel Management and Industrial Relations, Tata Institute of Social Sciences.

Sands, R. G. (1982). Styles of consciousness among industrial workers: A concern for industrial social work. *Arete*, 7 (1), 11-22.

Sarin, E. (1990). Elton Mayo and the experiences of Western Electric. *L'Annee Sociologique*, 40 (1), 287-311.

Sarkar, S. (2004). Industrial social work to corporate social responsibility: Is it a shift in object from curbing loss to making profit? *Indian Journal of Industrial Relations*, 40 (2), 273-284.

Sati, P. N. (1972). Democratization of industries and the place of industrial social worker. *Social Work Forum*, 10 (2), 3-13.

Savita, K. (2005). Future of HR: Role of social work education. *Social Work Review*, special issue, 66-73.

Saxena, A. (2004). Social work in industry: Knowledge, attitudes and practices of HR functionaries in Gujarat:

Social work perspective (an empirical study). *Social Work Review*, special issue, 53-60.

Saxena, A. (2005). Social work in industry: Implications on social work education, knowledge, attitudes and practices of HR functionaries in Gujarat: Social work perspective (an empirical study). *Social Work Review*, special issue, 89-99.

Scheuer, S. (1994). *HRM under collective bargaining: The sociological perspective*. USA: International Sociological Association (ISA).

Schneider, R. J., & Colan, N. B. (1992). The effectiveness of employee assistance programme supervisor training: An experimental study. *Human Resource Development Quarterly*, 3 (4), 345-356.

Schore, L., & Atkin, J. (1993). Stress in the workplace: A response from union member assistance programmes. In Kurzman, P.A., & Akabas, S.H. (Eds.), *Work and well-being: The occupational social work advantage*. (pp.316-331). Washington, DC: NASW.

Seema, S. (2002). The problem with sex. *Business Today*, 90-92.

Sehgal, R. (1990). *Social work in industry: Problems and practices of personnel/welfare functionaries*. Ph.D. Thesis, Indore School of Social Work, Devi Ahilya University.

Sehgal, R. (2005). Social work and industry: Dilemma of partnership. *Contemporary Social Work*, 22, 47-63.

Shah, A. (2000). Mainstreaming the corporate initiatives in social development: Insights from experiences in Gujarat. *Social Change*, 30 (3&4), 88.

Shain, M., & Groeneveld, (1980). *Employee assistance programmes: Philosophy, theory and practice*. Lexington, MA: Lexington Books.

Sharma, D., & Kamath, R. (2004). Quality control circles: A

case to import from industry to education. *The Indian Journal of Social Work*, 65 (2), 273-282.

Sharma, K.R. (1997). *Industrial Labour in India*. New Delhi: Atlantic Publishers and Distributors.

Sharma, R. (2004). Corporate social responsibility: An emerging area of social work. *Social Work Review*, special issue, 30-36.

Shetty, L.P. (1993). *An industry's approach to alcoholism and alcohol related problems*. Ph.D. thesis, Department of Social Work, Tata Institute of Social Sciences.

Siddiqui, H. Y. (1997). *Working with communities*. New Delhi: Hira Publications.

Siddiqui, S. (2004). Social work in industry: Challenges and dilemmas. *Social Work Review*, special issue, 102-106.

Siddqui, H.Y., & Sukhramani, N. (2001). Occupational social work in India. In Maiden R. P. (Ed.), *Global perspectives of occupational social work*. New York: Haworth Press, Inc.

Silver, I. (2001). Strategically legitimizing philanthropists' identity claims: Community organizations as key players in the making of corporate social responsibility. *Sociological Perspectives*, 44 (2), 233-252.

Silverman, D. (1968). Formal organizations or industrial sociology: Toward a social action analysis of organizations. *Sociology*, 2 (2), 221-238.

Simon, L.V., & Akabas, S.H. (1993). Women workers in high-risk public service: Tokens under stress. In Kurzman, P.A., & Akabas, S.H. (Eds.), *Work and well-being: The occupational social work advantage*. (pp.297-315). Washington, DC: NASW.

Simpson, I. H. (1989). The sociology of work: Where have the workers gone? *Social Forces*, 67 (3), 563-581.

Singh, S. (2004). Social work in industry: Issues and challenges. *Social Work Review*, special issue, 9-20.

Singh, S. (2005). Role of schools of social work in human resource education. *Social Work Review*, special issue, 1-10.

Singleton, J. (2004). Employed elder caregivers: The use of company-sponsored benefits. *Michigan Sociological Review*, 18, 82-107.

Sinha, D. (1960). Social and behavioural problems in Industry. The Indian Journal of Social Work, 21(3), 235-245.

Sinha, D. (1990). *A study of managements' perception regarding the role of social workers in industry*. M.Phil Dissertation, Department of Social Work, University of Delhi.

Sinha, D. (1998). Social work in business and industry: Challenges for the 21st century. *Perspectives in Social work*, 13(1), 12-18.

Sivananthiran, A., & Venkataratnam, C.S. (2002). *Labour and social issues in plantations in South Asia: Role of social dialogue*. New Delhi: International Labour Organization.

Sivananthiran, A., & Venkataratnam, C.S. (2003). *Prevention and settlement of disputes in India*. New Delhi: International Labour Organization & Indian Industrial Relations Association.

Skidmore, R. A. (1974). Social work practice in industry. *Social Work*, 19 (3); 280-286.

Spitzer, K., & Favorini, A. (1993). The emergence of external employee assistance programmes. In Kurzman, P.A., & Akabas, S.H. (Eds.), *Work and well-being: The occupational social work advantage*. (pp.350-371). Washington, DC: NASW

Solanki, J. (2005). HR in social sector. *Social Work Review*, special issue, 145-149.

Soler, M. S. (1957). The individual and the group in industrial labour: Review of the Hawthorne experiments. *Revista Internacional de Sociologia*, 15-60, 593-618.

Sonnenstuhl, J., & O'Donnell, E. J. (1980). EAPs: The why's and how's of planning them. *Personnel Administrator*, 25.

Srivatsava, B.N. (1969). An interview with a personnel officer. *Social Work Forum*, 2 (1), 23-26.

Srivatsava, M. (2004). Practical of ethics in modern organizations. *Social Work Review*, special issue, 21-29.

Srivastva, S.D. (1974). *Labour welfare in the cotton textile industry of Uttar Pradesh*. Ph.D. Thesis, Department of Sociology, University of Lucknow.

Srivastava, S.P. (1999). Addressing the future of professional social work in India. *The Indian Journal of Social Work*, 60(1), 118-139.

Srivastava, V. (2001). Women workers awareness level and correlates thereof: Reflecting the agenda of social work intervention. *The Indian Journal of Social Work*, 62(2), 180-196.

Srinivasan, V. (1991). *Social work practice in industry: A study of manufacturing organizations in Madras*. Ph.D. Thesis, Department of Social Work, Tata Institute of Social Sciences.

Steiner, J. R., & Borst, E. C. C. (1980). Industrial settings: Underdeveloped opportunities for social work services. *Arete*, 6 (2), 1-11.

Steun, C., & Worden, D.B. (1993). The older worker and service delivery at the workplace. In Kurzman, P.A., & Akabas, S.H. (Eds.), *Work and well-being: The occupational social work advantage*. (pp.256-275). Washington, DC: NASW.

Stoesz, D. (1989). Human service corporations: New opportunities for administration in social work. *Administration in Social Work*, 13 (3-4), 183-197.

Straussner, S. L. A. (1988a). Comparison of in-house and contracted-out employee assistance programmes. *Social Work*, 33 (1), 53-55.

Straussner, S.L.A., & Phillips, N.K. (1988b). The relationship between social work and labour unions: A history of strife and cooperation. *Journal of Sociology and Social Welfare*, 15 (1), 105-118.

Straussner, S.A. (Ed.), (1990). *Occupational social work today*. New York: The Haworth Press, Inc.

Sundar, P. (2000). *Beyond business: From merchant charity to corporate citizenship*. New Delhi: Tata McGraw Hill Publishing Company Limited.

Susan, B., Michelle, F., & Richard, W. (1981). *Confidentiality issues in workplace settings*. New York: Industrial Social Welfare Center, Columbia University School of Social Work.

Tata Council for Community Initiatives. (2000). *Guidelines for community development*. Mumbai: Tata Services Limited.

Tata Council for Community Initiatives. (2002). *Tatas in the environment*. Mumbai: Tata Services Limited.

Tata Council for Community Initiatives. (2003). *Tata volunteers report*. Mumbai: Tata Services Limited.

Tata, N. H. (1953). Philosophies of labour welfare. *The Indian Journal of Social Work*, 14 (1), 37-41

Teare, J. R. (1987). *Occupational social work: An annotated bibliography*. Washington DC: NASW

Thakore, B.J. (2005). HR issues and challenges in different sectors: Business and service with a professional social work touch. *Social Work Review*, special issue, 25-30.

Thomas, P.T. (1967). Problems of social work education in India. *The Indian Journal of Social Work*, 28 (1), 41-54.

Thomilson, R.J. (Ed.), (1983a). *Perspectives in industrial social work practice*. Ottawa, Canada: Family Service Canada Publications.

Thomlison, R. J. (1983b). Setting the stage for industrial social work. In Thomlison, R J. (Ed.), *Perspectives on industrial social work practice*. (pp. 1-28). Canada: Family Service Canada Publications.

Tietze, S., & Musson,G. (2002). When "work" meets home': Temporal flexibility as lived experience. *Time and Society*, 11 (2-3), 315-334.

Tsui, S.M., & Chan, R.K.H. (1999). The future of social work: A revision and a vision. *The Indian Journal of Social Work*, 60(1), 87-98.

Tudiver, Neil. (1982). Business ideology and management in social work: The limits of cost control. *Catalyst*, 4, 1(13), 25-48.

University Grants Commission. (1990). *An Overview of Similarities and Peculiarities in Professional Social Work Education at PG and UG Educational Levels*. The Report of the Curriculum Development Centre in Social Work Education, New Delhi.

Upadhyay, R.K. (2003). *Social casework: A therapeutic approach*. Jaipur: Rawat Publications.

Vaid, K. N. (1959). Social work in industry. *Sociale Wetenschappen*, 2 (4), 238-251

Vaid, K.N. (1963). Personnel management and social work. *The Indian Journal of Social Work*, 24 (2), 134-136.

Van, B. P. (1968). Sociology without workers. *Sociologische Gids*, 15 (1), 2-13.

Van, B. A. D. (1999a). Developing resilience to routine separations: An occupational social work intervention. *Families in Society*, 80 (6), 597-605.

Vaudecranne. (1958). Summary of group discussions on professional preparation of personnel for social work in industry and the public services. *International Social Work* 1(1), 18-20.

Ved, G. K. (1953). Philosophies of labour welfare. *The Indian Journal of Social Work*, 14 (1), 54-58.

Verma, R.B.S. (2005). Course on human resource management in department/institution of social work. *Social Work Review*, special issue, 44-56.

Verma, R.P. (1970). *Labour welfare in Jamshedpur*. Ph.D. Thesis, Department of Economics, University of Ranchi.

Vigilante, W.F. (1993). Work: Its use in assessment and intervention with clients in the workplace. In Kurzman, P.A., & Akabas, S.H. (Eds.), *Work and well-being: The occupational social work advantage*. (pp.179-199). Washington, DC: NASW.

Vinton, L., & White, B. (1995). The "boutique effect" in graduate social work education. *Journal of Teaching in Social Work*, 11 (1-2), 3-13.

Vishwanathan, N. (1963). Social work in industry. *Indian Journal of Social Work*, 24 (2), 62-68.

Vyas, M.D., & Bulchandani, A. (2004). Quality of work life. *Social Work Review*, special issue, 120-124.

Wagner, M. (1983). Trauma counselling and law enforcement. In Thomlison, R.J. (Ed.), *Perspectives on industrial social work practice*. (pp. 133-139). Canada: Family Service Canada Publications.

Watson, T. (1980). Sociology, work and industry. London: Routledge & Keganpaul Publications.

Wenocur, S., & Reisch, M. (1989). *From Charity to enterprise: The development of American social work in a market economy*. Urbana, Illinois: University of Illinois Press.

Weissman, A. (1975). A social service strategy in industry. *Social Work*, 20 (5), 401-402.

Whyte, W. F. (1965). Industrial sociology: A field in search of a focus. *Industrial and Labour Relations Review*, 18 (3), 305-322.

Whyte, W. F. (1956). Problems of industrial sociology. *Social Problems*, 4 (2), 148-160.

Witvrouw, M. (1958). Professional preparation of personnel

for social work in industry and the public services. *International Social Work,* 1(1), 10-18.

Wood, S. (1981). Industrial sociology in practice. *The Sociological Review,* 29 (2), 271-282.

Woods, R., & Maenetja, T. (1996). Occupational social work in profit-driven enterprises: Issues for social work education in South Africa in the late 1990s. *Maatskaplike Werk/Social Work,* 32 (2), 112-122.

Wright, D. (1983). Marketing, planning and implementation of industrial social work programmes. In Thomlison, R. J. (Ed.), *Perspectives on industrial social work practice.* (pp. 47-56). Canada: Family Service Canada Publications.

Wyers, L. N., & Kaulukukui Malina. (1984). Social Services in the workplace: rhetoric vs. reality. *Social Work,* 29, 167-172.

Yamatani, H. (1988). Client assessment in an industrial setting: A cross-sectional method. *Social work,* 33, 34-37.

Zapusek, D. (1998). Models of social work at Velenje Mines. *Socialno Delo,* 37 (3-5), 291-294.

Zundel, E. (1972). Social work in the factory. *Kolner Zeitschrift fur Soziologie und Sozialpsychologie,* 24 (2), 282-300.

Web Sites:

www.avenueconsulting.co.uk

www.tiss.edu

www.fetchinfo.com

www.indianngos.com

www.nasw.com

www.tatatea.com

www.tcs.com

www.titanworld.com

www.tataref.com

www.tatasteel.com
www.worldcatlibraries.org
www.tatamotors.com
www.tatainfotech.com
www.tatacentralarchives.com

Index